PENGUIN MODERN CLASSICS

Selected Poems

KAMALA DAS (1934–2009) was a major Indian English poet and an important Malayalam writer. She was born into a distinguished literary family. Her mother, Balamani Amma, was a well-known Malayalam poet and her grand-uncle Nalapat Narayana Menon was a renowned writer and translator. She grew up in Punnayurkulam, her ancestral village in Kerala, and in Calcutta where her parents lived. She was married off at the age of fifteen, and began writing and publishing while in her teens. With her taboo-breaking early poetry and her controversial autobiography, Kamala became an icon for Indian women. In English, she published six collections of poetry in her lifetime—*Summer in Calcutta* (1965), *The Descendants* (1967), *The Old Playhouse and Other Poems* (1973), *Collected Poems* vol. I (1984), *Only the Soul Knows How to Sing: Selections from Kamala Das* (1996), *Encountering Kamala* (2007)—and her autobiography, *My Story* (1976). She was recognized with many literary prizes, including the Sahitya Akademi and the Vayalar awards.

DEVINDRA KOHLI was Professor of English at the University of Kashmir, Srinagar, a Visiting Professor at universities in Germany, including Bonn, Duisburg-Essen, Frankfurt and Münster. He was a Foundation Fellow, Clare Hall, Cambridge; a Henry Chapman Fellow, University of London; and a Chancellor's International Lecturer, University of Missouri-St Louis. Author of *Kamala Das* (1975), he has edited/co-edited *Indian Writers at Work*, *Contemporary Indian Short Stories*, *Anita Desai: Essays in Interpretation*, and contributed to the *Times Literary Supplement*, the *Journal of Commonwealth Literature*, the *Malahat Review*, *Gravesiana* and *Wasafiri*.

PENGUIN MODERN CLASSICS

Selected Poems

KAMALA DAS (1934–2009) was a major Indian English poet and a major Malayalam writer. She was born into a distinguished literary family. Her mother, Balamani Amma, was a well-known Malayalam poet and her grand-uncle Nalapat Narayana Menon was a renowned writer and translator. She grew up in Punnayurkulam, her ancestral village in Kerala, and in Calcutta where her parents lived. She was married off at the age of fifteen, and began writing and publishing while in her teens. With her ground-breaking early poetry and her controversial autobiography, Kamala became an icon for Indian women. In English, she published six collections of poetry in her lifetime—*Summer in Calcutta* (1965), *The Descendants* (1967), *The Old Playhouse and Other Poems* (1973), *Collected Poems*, vol. 1 (1984), *Only the Soul Knows How to Sing: Selections from Kamala Das* (1996), *Yaa Allah*, *Encountering Kamala* (2007)—and her autobiography, *My Story* (1976). She was recognized with many literary prizes, including the Sahitya Akademi and the Vayalar Awards.

DEVINDRA KOHLI was Professor of English at the University of Kashmir, Srinagar, a Visiting Professor at universities in Germany, including Bonn, Duisburg-Essen, Frankfurt and Münster. He was a Foundation Fellow, Clare Hall, Cambridge; a Henry Chapman Fellow, University of London; and a Chancellor's International Lecturer, University of Missouri–St Louis. Author of *Kamala Das* (1975), he has edited *Indian Writers at Work*, *Contemporary Indian Short Stories*, *Anita Desai: Essays in Introduction*, and contributed to the *Times Literary Supplement*, the *Journal of Commonwealth Literature*, the *Malahat Review*, *Overland* and *Wasafiri*.

KAMALA DAS

Selected Poems

Edited with an Introduction by Devindra Kohli

PENGUIN BOOKS
An imprint of Penguin Random House

PENGUIN BOOKS

USA | Canada | UK | Ireland | Australia
New Zealand | India | South Africa | China | Singapore

Penguin Books is part of the Penguin Random House group of companies whose addresses can be found at global.penguinrandomhouse.com

Published by Penguin Random House India Pvt. Ltd
4th Floor, Capital Tower 1, MG Road,
Gurugram 122 002, Haryana, India

Penguin Random House India

First published by Penguin Books India 2014

10 9 8 7 6 5 4 3 2

ISBN 9780143421047

Typeset in Dante MT Std by Eleven Arts, Delhi

Printed at Manipal Technologies Limited, India

www.penguin.co.in

FSC www.fsc.org MIX Paper from responsible sources FSC® C043100

This is a legitimate digitally printed version of the book and therefore might not have certain extra finishing on the cover.

Contents

From *The Descendants* (1967)

From *The Old Playhouse and Other Poems* (1973)

From *Closure* (2009)

Introduction

> I am obnoxious to each carping tongue,
> Who says my hand a needle better fits;
> A poet's pen all scorn I should thus wrong,
> For such despite they cast on female wits;
> If what I do prove well, it won't advance,
> They'll say it's stol'n, or else it was by chance.
>
> —Anne Bradstreet (1612–72)

Kamala Das and the Spirit of the 1960s

In 1964, Kamala Das won the Poetry Prize of the Asian PEN anthology sponsored by the Philippine branch, and with the prize money, she tells us, she opened her personal bank account at the age of thirty. Her poems had been appearing in the journal of the *Indian PEN* (edited by Sophia Wadia, Bombay) since the 1950s when she sent them her first poem. Her first collection of fifty poems, *Summer in Calcutta* (1965), was a landmark book. Kamala Das's homespun style—her speech rhythms, with their almost total disregard of the traditional iambic line of English verse, her imagery drawn from immediate contexts of experience, her individual tone of voice at times assuming a 'loud poster' persona and yet disarmingly owning and sometimes playing on 'its distortions, its queernesses'—struck a refreshingly new chord in English poetry in India. With the two subsequent volumes, *The Descendants* (1967) and *The Old Playhouse and Other Poems* (1973), her poetry opened up new possibilities both in content and style.

As Eunice de Souza puts it, 'Women writers owe a special debt to Kamala Das. She mapped out the terrain for postcolonial women in social and linguistic terms'.[1] Other poets who have acknowledged her contribution include Meena Alexander, Rukmini Bhaya Nair, Shirley Geok-lin Lim, Carol Rumens, R. Parthasarathy, Jeet Thayil, Hoshang Merchant, Suresh Kohli, Tishani Doshi and Meena Kandasamy.

Historically, like the recognition accorded to Nissim Ezekiel and Dom Moraes, that given to Kamala Das as a significant contemporary Indian poet in English is also a reflection of the political, cultural and literary changes in the 1960s and 1970s that impacted those of us who received or gave English literary education both within and outside India. It was these changes that had made *An Anthology of Commonwealth Verse* (1963) possible: a groundbreaking selection of 234 poets from the British Isles and the Commonwealth countries that included Kamala Das among thirty pre- and post-Independence Indian poets. In her introduction, Margaret O'Donnell, the editor, lauded their contribution not only 'to their own truly national culture' but '*more important*, to the broad development of English literature'[2] (italics mine). This perspective signified a major shift in the way literary and cultural critics had begun to view Anglophone writers, male and female, from a non-white, non-Western background. From a critical perspective, therefore, O'Donnell's anthology was a recognition of cultural difference and diversity that obtained in the English verse written, for example, by Indian and Pakistani poets such as Aurobindo, Sarojini Naidu, Nissim Ezekiel, P. Lal, Dom Moraes, Kamala Das, Suhrawardy and Zulfikar Ghose.

The international recognition accorded to the legitimacy of diversity had been triggered by the complex interrelated, radical changes in politics, art, literature and technology that took place across the globe during the 'cultural decade' which extended up to the mid-1970s, and is also popularly known as the High Sixties. The Civil Rights Movement in 1963 in the US led by Martin Luther King Jr, inspired by Gandhi, whom he called 'the guiding light', resonated in other countries because, significantly, during the same decade thirty-two African countries attained independence from colonial rule. This resonance was also evident in the literary realm, in the transnational reception of non-Western poets and novelists such as Chinua Achebe, Wole Soyinka, Amos Tutuola, Derek Walcott and V.S. Naipaul, whose work focused in particular on interrogating race, colour and identity.

When the Civil Rights Act of 1964 was amended in the US to include gender, it politicized the movement for women's rights that had already been spearheaded by such writers as Betty Friedan who, in *The Feminine Mystique* (1963), had questioned the received ideals of women's roles and the problematic nature of identity. The exploration of aspects of gender identity and empowerment increasingly became the focus of a number of women writers, both white and non-white, such as Gwendolyn Brooks, Maya Angelou, Sylvia Plath, Jean Rhys, Toni Morrison, Kate Millett and Germaine Greer. The old notions of hierarchy and authority in politics, culture and family were being questioned in the language of a counterculture.

This increasing openness to cultural difference and diversity was coupled with a desire for innovation and experimentation, as is evident in the impact of Indian music and philosophy on Allen Ginsberg, the Beat poets and the Beatles. While in England, George Harrison was making a daring experiment in cultural fusion by uncannily complementing his sitar with John Lennon's guitar to weave the magic of 'Norwegian Wood'; in the US, Bob Dylan, through his protest songs, was reminding writers, critics, and lawmakers, 'who prophesize with your pen', to 'keep your eyes wide . . . / For the times they are a-changin'. Was this kind of liberating voice, questioning middle-class values, a common feature of the social change in the High Sixties? Philip Larkin described the year 1963, using the tone of 'a non-literal satire on the 1960s in general', as a sort of personal annus mirabilis when 'sexual intercourse began . . . / Between the end of the "Chatterley" ban / And the Beatles' first LP'.

In his description of the circle of innovative Indian poets in Bombay during the early 1960s of which he was a member, Adil Jussawalla remarks that 'there was a considerable influence of the Beats';[3] and Arvind Krishna Mehrotra, another member of the circle, recalls the impact of Andy Warhol and 'hippie' and avant-garde art experiments intended 'to erase the boundaries between art and ordinary speech, or art and cardboard boxes, or art and fart . . .'[4] 'Innocent of formal education' and of such spirited modernist experiments, Kamala Das's affinities were with the nineteenth-century Whitman and the instinct behind her poetry was, even though it was not formally articulated, precisely to erase the boundaries between poetry and ordinary speech, and to write in recognizable speech rhythms of the poet herself.

O'Donnell's anthology provided timely ferment for a conceptual shift towards the inclusion of non-Western writers in the canon of English literary studies at universities throughout the world. It was not, however, the very first publication in this field: it was preceded by A.L. McLeod's pioneering 'introduction to one [lesser known] aspect of English literature' in *The Commonwealth Pen: An Introduction to the Literature of the British Commonwealth* (1961), an endorsement in the special 'Language in Common' issue of the *Times Literary Supplement* (10 August 1962), and followed by Joseph Jones's *Terranglia:*

The Case for English as a World Literature (1965). Although the term Commonwealth Literature is no longer widely used today, and has been subsumed under labels such as Postcolonial and Transnational Literatures, it is significant that the first international conference on Commonwealth Literature was held in 1964 at the University of Leeds in England; subsequently, the *Journal of Commonwealth Literature* was started and this was followed by the journal of *World Literature Written in English* in the US in 1966.

In India, this shift in canon at universities was pioneered by K.R. Srinivasa Iyengar (1908–99), and C.D. Narasimhaiah (1921–2005) whose journal, the *Literary Criterion*, provided a forum for what seems, in retrospect, to be a postcolonial counterpoint to the traditional canon of English studies. The curriculum of English studies at Indian universities in the sixties was still predominantly an Anglo-American curriculum. The debate over whether an authentic Indian literature could be written in English at all that reigned strongly then has by no means come to an end today, but the fact that in 1967 the *Literary Criterion* published a full-length article on Kamala Das's first book of poems, *Summer in Calcutta* (1965),[5] was an encouraging sign of the changing paradigm in the critical reception of Indian poetry in English in India.

At a time when there were few outlets for publishing poetry in book form except by the Writers Workshop in Calcutta, the stimulus from the *Illustrated Weekly of India* and C.R. Mandy, its Irish editor, the *Indian PEN* and *Quest* in Bombay, the *Miscellany* in Calcutta, and *Thought* in Delhi was very important. Among the poets C.R. Mandy published in the *Illustrated Weekly* were Nissim Ezekiel, P. Lal, Dom Moraes and Kamala Das. Kamala Das served as the *Weekly*'s poetry editor on two occasions: between 1971 and 1972, and 1978 and 1979.

Equally important were the roles that Nissim Ezekiel and P. Lal played as mentors and guides to the younger poets. The 1960s also saw the birth of several interesting, however short-lived, avant-garde magazines such as *damn you: a magazine of the arts* and *Ezra: an imagiste magazine*. These magazines were edited by new poets themselves and they affirmed the influence of the English modernists such as Ezra Pound and T.S. Eliot. Although Kamala Das was not associated with any such group during her long years in Bombay, she herself founded and ran Bahutantrika, a monthly forum for poets, playwrights and artists who met at her flat for readings and performances.

For Indian poets writing in English, the cry was for change and innovation. To them, the themes and language of the eminent pre-1947 poets such as Aurobindo, Sarojini Naidu and Tagore (in his Nobel Prize–winning English rendering of *Gitanjali*), who were inspired and shaped by the Indian freedom movement, seemed remote. Aurobindo had been inspired by Milton's seventeenth-century epic, *Paradise Lost*. Just as Milton, in his time, had been imprisoned for his republican alliance with Cromwell, Aurobindo was also imprisoned by the British for his nationalist activism. Like Milton, Aurobindo had not only been educated at Cambridge but was also a scholar of Greek and Latin. Milton meant his epic to be 'doctrinal and exemplary to a nation'; Aurobindo, too, had intended his *Savitri*, based on the tale of married love between Satyavan and Savitri in the Mahabharata, to serve a similar national function. Therefore, for Aurobindo, the freedom-fighter-turned-spiritualist, accomplishing an Indian epic in the blank verse of Shakespeare and Milton, had been a case of 'the Empire writes back with a [sweet] vengeance', to use Salman Rushdie's metaphor coined in 1982 which has become a benchmark of the postcolonial writer.

It is clear that the Aurobindo model of poet as national prophet or that of Sarojini Naidu as nationalist nightingale, writing in blank and/or rhymed verse to emulate the style of their English counterparts, was at odds with most of the post-Independence Indian poets, whether it was Kamala Das, or Ezekiel and the group of poets in Bombay such as Adil Jussawalla, R. Parthasarathy, Keki Daruwalla and Arvind Krishna Mehrotra, or P. Lal and the poets associated with the Writers Workshop in Calcutta. The real issues, themes and sensibilities of independent India were to be understood and dealt with in other ways.

The new models for most of the post-Independence Indian poets in English, who were university educated and/or university teachers, were contemporary British and American modernist poets like Ezra Pound and T.S. Eliot who had also rejected Milton and much of Romantic and Victorian poetry as being out of tune with their times. 'Make it new' and 'break the pentameter' is what Ezra Pound and the imagists such as Amy Lowell had urged; and Eliot, too, had experimented with free verse. However, modernism, whether in English, American or Indian anglophone poetry, is a complex issue and does not mean an outright rejection of the English iambic line, as is evident in the poems of Ezekiel and Dom Moraes in the 1960s and 1970s. This is also evident today in the poetry of Vikram Seth.[6] Thus R.W. Desai's lament over the lack of 'the sculpture of rhyme', using a phrase of Pound's, in his critique of two anthologies of Indian poetry in English reflected the dominant critical influence in university departments of English.[7]

In order to articulate the cadences and stresses of a non-English sensibility, however, as the Irish poet Seamus Heaney has pointed out, the English iambic line needs to be 'wrecked' at times because 'the voice itself, the authenticating energy and melody, is not from the tradition but comes out of the genius of the writer himself'.[8] Amy Lowell had remarked that 'the individuality of a poet may often be better expressed in free-verse than in conventional forms. In poetry a new cadence means a new idea.' Free verse, as long as it was not undisciplined, would allow the Indian poets the flexibility to use their own distinctive cadences of speech and the force and originality of their image patterns, given their regional, linguistic, cultural variety and different speech rhythms; the traditional English iambic line would not be adequate for this purpose. And 'the pig-headed father' of 'free verse' with whom Ezra Pound made a 'truce' was Walt Whitman whom Kamala Das discovered as a kindred spirit while, as a young girl, she browsed in the library of her grand-uncle, the poet and scholar Nalapat Narayana Menon.

Having signalled the need to break fresh personal ground in *A Time to Change* (1952), his first book of poems, Ezekiel was speaking for the new Indian sensibility in 'Morning Prayer' (included in O'Donnell's *Anthology*) where he pleads with God in his nuanced ironic humour to grant him 'the fresh inward eye' and 'Restore my waking time / To vital present tense'. Given his seminal experience of England, Ezekiel, like Dom Moraes, voiced his 'vital present tense' through impressive experimentation with the English iambic line. Kamala Das, on the other hand, flouted the iambic line and wove her own unconventional line, homespun verbal tapestry to accommodate and dignify her 'vernacular oddities' and capture 'the speech of the mind that is / Here and not there, a mind that sees and hears and / Is aware'.

During the four decades since O'Donnell's *An Anthology of Commonwealth Verse*, Indian poetry in English had made radical departures in poetic style in the work of poets such as Adil Jussawalla, Jayanta Mahapatra, Arvind Krishna Mehrotra and

Arun Kolatkar. As the poet Jeet Thayil notes, with 'the psychic weather that poets such as A.K. Ramanujan, Keki Daruwalla, Eunice de Souza and R. Parthasarathy brought to their lines' that Internationalism established itself on the English page in India . . .'[9] The psychic weather that Kamala Das brought to her lines, and thereby to Indian poetry in English is also a part of this international space even though it came by a different and a less formally and academically oriented route.

Was there, then, a symbiosis during the 1960s and 1970s between post-Independence Indian English poetry and its critical recognition? In 1969, P. Lal brought out *Modern Indian Poetry in English: An Anthology and a Credo*, rather overgenerously showcasing 134 contributors, and Saleem Peeradina's anthology *Contemporary Indian Poetry in English: An Assessment and Selection* appeared in 1972. Between 1970 and 1976, the *Journal of Commonwealth Literature* published seven articles and reviews on Indian poetry in English.[10] When Oxford University Press, India, launched its Three Crowns series with *Ten Twentieth-Century Indian Poets*, edited by R. Parthasarathy, and collections of poems by Nissim Ezekiel, A.K. Ramanujan and Keki Daruwalla, and Arnold-Heinemann brought out critical studies of Nissim Ezekiel and Kamala Das in the Indian Writers series in the early 1970s, it seemed that Indian poetry in English had arrived 'officially' in India in terms of its international reception, first signalled by O'Donnell's *An Anthology of Commonwealth Verse*.

However, post-Independence Indian English writers have been criticized by writers in other Indian languages more than they were in pre-Independence India. In 1965, when new poetry was being published by Nissim Ezekiel, Dom Moraes and Kamala Das, there was, ironically, in Bombay, a chauvinist movement of anti-colonial protest. Kala Ghoda, the black granite equestrian statue of King Edward VII, symbolizing the colonial space of the crowded south Bombay, was vandalized by the adherents of the so-called nationalist movement. In 1963, the year in which O'Donnell's anthology was published, *The Concise Encyclopedia of English and American Poets and Poetry* (eds Stephen Spender and Donald Hall) carried an essay by the eminent Bengali author Buddhadeva Bose in which he debunked modern Indian poetry in English as 'a blind alley, lined with curio shops, leading nowhere'. P. Lal's 1969 anthology was, in fact, launched as a rejoinder to Buddhadeva Bose.[11] In 2002, several eminent Indian-language writers, including Sunil Gangopadhyay, Dilip Chitre and Bhalchandra Nemade, variously described Indian writers in English as 'creative travel writers', 'artificial western flowers', 'necromancers, creating something out of nothing', and dismissed their writing as contingent on 'an English language mirror to know its face', or simply overvalued 'just like a fair-skinned woman [is] in our society'.[12]

The comparison of the overprized fair-skinned woman with Indian writing or writers in English, although seemingly metaphorical, reflects a real undercurrent of social ambivalence in India. In the same survey cited above, the late Nirmal Verma, a distinguished Hindi writer and a sensitive reader of English, comparing language to a bride, deplored Indian writers in English who by choosing a wrong bride ended up 'in a strange place' with 'the emotional content' and 'the real core of the Indian experience' missing.[13] In asserting her freedom to write in English, as a 'very brown' trilingual Indian and a bilingual woman writer from south India, Kamala Das not only claimed her postcolonial space but also her national space in a multilingual India against a perceptible colourism that impacts women.

'With Its Quiet Tongue', the poem by Kamala Das which

O'Donnell included in *An Anthology of Commonwealth Verse*, is a 'dialogue' of a woman with herself, reflecting on the tension between a failed love in or outside of marriage and the expected fortitudinous silence of an Indian woman, or for that matter any woman, as Keats, although using it in a different context of the art–life paradigm, implied in his memorable phrase 'unravished bride of quietness'. Kamala Das's poem offers no resolution or closure but it breaks the traditional silence instead of mirroring it. It enacted the paradigm of the Indian housewife as poet, ten years before the American feminist poet and novelist Erica Jong was to outline her aesthetic of 'The Artist as Housewife: The Housewife as Artist'.[14]

In choosing English rather than Malayalam, Kamala was also subverting the traditional male paradigm of woman as Muse implicit in Nirmal Verma's metaphor of language as 'bride', and as I shall show in a subsequent section, she was claiming, as a woman poet, her own version of the Muse. She claimed her space by refusing to conform to socially defined roles, even while fulfilling them, and in the process reinvented herself, and at times deliberately blurred the line between life and poetry, only to offer another paradox: 'It's my poems that are my life, and not my prose.'

The Making of an Icon Who Was Also an Iconoclast

Kamala Das was born on 31 March 1934 into an aristocratic Nalapat Nair family in Punnayurkulam of Thrissur district in Kerala, also known as the Malabar region. Her maternal grandmother was the daughter of the Raja of Punnathurkotta and was married to the Raja of Chittanjoor. Her mother, Balamani Amma (1909–2004), a distinguished poet in Malayalam, had, after an arranged marriage at the age of nineteen in 1928, moved to Calcutta where her husband, Vadakkekkara Madhavan Nair (1896–1977), worked in the Walford Transport Company which sold Bentleys, Rolls-Royces and Humbers.

Subsequently, he became the managing director and managing editor of the *Mathrubhumi Weekly* and settled in Kerala. According to Kamala Das, as her grandfather was financially broke at the time, the family had to shed their 'caste snobbery' in favour of the financially secure V.M. Nair and accept an 'unthinkable' arrangement of a Nalapat girl marrying a man who was neither a royal nor a Brahmin.[15]

Kamala, too, had an arranged marriage. In February 1949, at the age of fifteen, she was married off to Kalipurayath Madhava Das (1920–92), who worked in the Reserve Bank of India in Bombay, a specialist in economics and rural credit projects. In 1966 he collaborated with Eleanor Margaret Hough in preparing the fifth and revised edition of her book *The Co-operative Movement in India*. While Kamala disliked her husband's submersion in office work even at home, she warmly remembered Eleanor Hough, his 'affectionate friend', visiting their 'pokey flat at Dadar for tea'.

> On our oldest sofa, loose-limbed and relaxed, playing with my infant son . . . She was about sixty then, with white streaks in her hair and wrinkles beneath her eyes. In her movements she displayed the pliancy of a rag doll. But there was a vigour in her glance which made her attractive.[16]

Before her marriage, Kamala Das was tutored at home and studied at the St Cecilia European Catholic School in Calcutta. She never went to university. She spent her summer vacations at her ancestral house in Punnayurkulam in Malabar where she had developed a close bond with her grandmother who was 'the demonstrative kind, unlike my parents who believed in observing restraint in every kind of emotional outlay'.[17] Kamala Das had a keen observing eye and a flair for the theatre, painting and writing. She also had a rare gift of empathy: at six, she was composing 'sad poems about dolls who lost their heads and had to remain headless for eternity'. When she was twelve her short story 'Kushtarogi' (The Leper) was published in 'Balapankhi', the children's section of the *Mathrubhumi Weekly*, followed by 'Avalude Katha' (Her Story) in the main section, and by 'Stree' (Woman) in June 1947 under her given name. However, with her story 'Puzha Veendum Ozhuki' (And Again Flowed the River), published in June 1953, she adopted the pseudonym Madhavikutty (the child wife of Madhava, as she explains)[18] because she did not want her love stories to shock her 'puritan' grandmother. It was about the same time that she began writing poems in English and had her first poem published in the *Indian PEN* magazine.

After her marriage in 1949, Kamala Das lived largely in Bombay where her husband was posted until 1981, except for a spell each in Calcutta and Delhi when he was on secondment. It was during her stay in Delhi in the early sixties, when her husband was posted at the Planning Commission, that *Summer in Calcutta* was published. She had made friends with writers and playwrights, including Rajinder Paul (1940–91) of Everest Press, 'a drama critic, a young man who resembled Mark Antony in his looks', and editor and publisher of *Enact*, a theatre monthly magazine (now defunct), to which Kamala Das contributed one-act plays and theatre reviews.[19]

Before she came to Delhi there had been inner turmoil for Kamala Das, a nervous breakdown, followed by psychiatric help, and a longish stay in Malabar. After her return to Delhi from Calicut, her health continued to deteriorate and she was hospitalized. When her husband's secondment in Delhi ended, the family returned to Bombay in 1966 and, after a short stay at Cadell Road, they settled in a spacious flat in Bank House, Backbay Reclamation, Churchgate, near 'the sprawling Sachivalaya', with the sea, as 'our neighbour'.

It seems to have been perhaps the most troubled period of her life when, at times, she found herself doubting the reality of the world outside; she wrote poems and painted pictures which 'showed demons mating with snakes'.[20] Recently independent India was shaken in 1962 by the sirens of political and military conflict with China, and with Pakistan in 1965 and in 1971. These sirens are heard in her one-act play *The Fourteen Days' War*, published in *Enact*, but she seems to have been 'unnerved' by another kind of 'siren's baby-wail'.[21] Reflecting on her own 'scars of operations', she had spectres of death haunting 'the old playhouse of my mind, in its echoing hollowness'. As room no. 565 of a Bombay hospital became a familiar site, 'like a homecoming', as she put it, and the idea of writing about her experiences was mooted by her doctor as a curative diversion, the frenetic narrative of her autobiography took hold of her. She accepted the offer of the *Malayalnadu*, a popular (now defunct) Malayalam weekly in which *Ente Katha* was first serialized in 1972; it was published in book form in 1973. The longer English version, *My Story*, was serialized in 1974 in the *Current Weekly* and published in book form in 1976. Going by textual evidence, it can be argued that Kamala Das had actually intended or preferred to write her story in verse much earlier. Her later foray into writing columns for various magazines and newspapers such as *Femina* and *Savvy* were the inevitable consequence and extension of her first venture into non-fictional prose, with *Ente Katha/My*

Story undertaken largely for financial compulsion. She always saw herself only as poet and short-story writer, and maintained till the end that she wrote poetry for herself and prose only for money.

The response to her fiercely outspoken portrayal of the emotional and sexual life of a middle-class housewife was generally hostile and hypocritical, especially in Kerala and in urban middle-class settings; even in cosmopolitan cities it was marked by prurient curiosity. This disturbed her even though she was not surprised. She stoutly resisted it when her father asked the editor to suspend the publication of her narrative. Subsequently, Kamala Das was obliged to disclaim the truth of her narrative and said that a part of her autobiography was fictional. This it probably was, since autobiography, too, is mediated by the imagination and involves an element of selection; however, she did not disown the 'unapologetic' preface to the English editions brought out by Sterling Publishers, which asserted her sense of relief at having unburdened herself for the sake of 'a scrubbed-out conscience'. This preface was dropped without an explanatory note in later editions.[22]

An autobiography written at thirty-seven is rather unusual, especially when the author is a housewife-poet, and as such would not be expected to have closure, either in a chronological or philosophical sense. *My Story*, however, ends on a mixed note, gloomy and hopeful, a hovering prospect of imminent disintegration buttressed by a belief in the permanence of things in their changing contours and contexts—the paradoxical notion of permanence in change.

One consequence of the mixed reception to *My Story* was Kamala Das's withdrawal from the social circle of non-writers and purveyors of middle-class respectability not only in Kerala but also in Bombay. In an unpublished poem, 'The Invisible Woman', she was no longer just 'a dangerous freak' who truthfully though flamboyantly confronted and explored a married woman's inner life but

> A flightless bird that employs its wings only in its dreams
> I am the one on whom the garlands fade, such is the heat
> Of my loneliness . . .
> . . .
> I a mere nobody outside my hospital
> The ladies with tight hair-do look through me, I have written
> Four hundred poems and have now become invisible . . .

'The safe anonymity of the cave' where she wrote stories and poems began, however, to feel claustrophobic. So she channelled her social and creative energies by founding Bahutantrika, 'a club of talents',[23] when every first Saturday of the month poets, playwrights, dancers, editors, and publishers gathered for readings and performances in the spacious living room of her Bank House apartment. For Kamala Das, 'this monthly fiesta' served a therapeutic, social and creative purpose:

> I must keep myself alive not only by eating the pills prescribed by my cardiologist but also by this monthly fiesta, this mood that we have decided to call the Bahutantrika. Each of these evenings makes me feel wanted . . . Without people, without the poetry readings and the music this home shall be a cold place.[24]

Given its open-house and many-faceted character, with coffee served 'in the chipped white cups of the M.L.A.'s hostel and two varieties of snacks', Bahutantrika was as far from becoming a coterie as Kamala Das herself was from being elitist. Her youngest son, Jaisurya Das, recalls growing up in that setting charged with literary activity: 'Our home was an open house and also one of the inspirations for my mother to carry on the great work.'[25]

As Kamala Das recounted, some writers including Saleem Peeradina and Darius Cooper attended Bahutantrika occasionally: Keki Daruwalla on one occasion 'inaugurated the session with a reading of his famous poem "The Harang" and the later one [unpublished then] on the city of Bombay'.[26] Randhir Khare, Suresh Kohli, Pritish Nandy who recalls it as 'a literary environment that was incredibly intense and magical', Shailaja Ganguly, Shobhaa Dé, Malavika Sangghvi, and Rukmini Bhaya Nair cherished it not only for 'the pheromone scent of her poems'[27] but also for Kamala Das's 'benign eye and impish encouragement'.[28]

When I first met her in her home in July 1978 for lunch with her mother, Balamani Amma, and Rita Glass, who later published a German translation of *My Story*,[29] it was clear that Kamala Das's enthusiasm for Bahutantrika was unmistakable. That was three years before she was to bid goodbye to Bombay. In her vignette three years thereafter, Shailaja Ganguly recalls the dynamics of Bahutantrika that many adored while Kamala's critics viewed it as 'exhibitionism', unsettling like the 'confessional' strain in her poetry and in *My Story*:

> Weighed down by the gold of Nalapat House, she held court like a queen in exile: cajoling a shy craftsman to face the crowd, presenting a well-known name with her inimitable flourish: planning quaint surprises (like a Sylvia Plath look-alike floating in from a balcony . . . scripting a skit to be enacted between two items of a Bharat Natyam recital. Or just clucking around happily pressing snacks or coffee on the floating crowd.[30]

Kamala Das, Bank House, near 'the sprawling Sachivalya', with the sea, as 'our neighbour'. July 1978, Bombay. Courtesy: Devindra Kohli.

Kamala Das, the editor, Rita Glass, Balamani Amma, and a friend of Kamala's. July 1978, Bank House, Bombay. Kamala's portrait on the wall and this photograph were drawn and taken by Herbert Willweber.

One creative outcome of the Bahutantrika bonhomie was Kamala Das's joint volume of poems, *Tonight, This Savage Rite*, with Pritish Nandy in 1979. As Kamala Das described the collaboration to me, Nandy's suggested modus operandi was that he would drop in and they would sit in different parts of the room and write poems. Not all of her seventeen new poems in *Tonight, This Savage Rite*, five of which are included in this selection, were the direct outcome of the arrangement with Nandy. *My Story* had earned her the reputation of being a 'liberated' woman, open to sexual adventure. In 1967 in her poem 'Composition', a part of which she interpolated in *My Story*, she had forewarned her readers: 'I am not yours for the asking.'

The success of *My Story* had come with a price. In 1972, four months after *Ente Katha* had begun to be serialized, she was invited to write a piece on pornography in Indian literature in which she asserted that while 'love is beautiful whatever four lettered name the puritans call it by . . . I am always too emotional to be pornographic.'[31] A closer look at both her autobiography and her love poems should deceive no one that her focus is on love, not on sex, although sex is seen as a part of it. In a conversation with me she mentioned that she had been dismissed as a fake or a compulsive fantasizer, since she had refused the overtures of some of her male acquaintances. In an unpublished poem entitled 'For Pritish' and dated 17 February 1975, Kamala Das says:

One of his girls told him that I was fake, that
No lover ever left his finger prints on me,
And together they laughed in their hotel bed, but
That was three years ago, she left him for another
And went away, he lost a lovely wife and son
Somewhere along the road, caught jaundice and the

Bitter fevers of the soul, but came again to
My city, my house, his belt wide as a poster,
His shirt unbuttoned to show his chest, dark, roughened
With hair, and I saw his eyes shrunken to slits,
The childish courage of his grin and felt that he
Had wrecked himself in hotel beds, floundered in the
Billows of stale sheets, struck against icebergs of words
While I remained safe, untouched by hand, the fake,
Yes, but they wore me like diamonds with pride, with joy.

Bahutantrika also gave Kamala her first brush with repressive politics. During the Emergency (1975–77) imposed by Prime Minister Indira Gandhi, these monthly cultural gatherings were perceived as encouraging anti-government writers to meet. Therefore, pressure was put on her even through her father, then president of the Indian Newspapers Society (1976–77), to discontinue them. Since she refused to comply, the police entered her home in 1976 in search of incriminating anti–Indira Gandhi material. In order to prevent her imminent arrest, the chief minister of Kerala, Achutha Menon, himself a writer, invited her to visit Kerala as a state guest and to prepare a report on the development of tourism in the state.

An unpublished poem, 'Darkness of a Sort', captures the different shades of the darkness of the presiding mood: 'the dark knot of fear' of the Emergency 'around / my heart' that sent her on a forced tourist mission, feeling rejected by her 'dear state' (for writing *My Story*) and returning to Bombay with 'a dark scab on my soul', the only redeeming dark being 'the eternal dusk' of the Kerala forests illumined by 'the shape of the lone tusker / looking ahead of me on / the mountain road above the Bison Valley'.

Indira Gandhi's government fell in March 1977. In a poem entitled 'Terror', Kamala Das memorialized the chilling nightmare of the Emergency, imagining 'our leader, leading us into / high exitless hills, standing tall / as a mountain goat upon the snow'.

In 1981 Kamala Das and her husband left Bombay after his retirement and settled in Trivandrum. She worked as the president of the Kerala Children's Film Society, a position which she enjoyed not only for the excitement which the work brought to her but also because it fulfilled a cherished dream of hers. In a letter of 23 November 1981, she wrote: 'I have a lovely feeling within me when I think of my job. I've always dreamt of being able to work but not academically qualified, was not lucky till now.' In the same letter, she expressed a sense of lyrical relief on leaving Bombay for good and returning to Kerala. For the next three years, however, since her husband was offered a bank consultancy in Sri Lanka, she divided her time between Trivandrum and Colombo. It was during this period that the ongoing ethnic conflict between the Sinhala nationalists and the Tamil population gained momentum; in July 1983, it turned into an armed civil war. While this forced many thousands of Tamils to leave the country, those living there lived in constant fear of a backlash. In a set of poems, appreciated as well as criticized, Kamala Das voiced her own sense of the ethnic conflict in Sri Lanka, and evoked the 'fear [that] had warped our movements' and how 'despite my nut brown skin', her attempts to 'merge well with the expatriates' had failed.

Yet, on the whole, her visits to Colombo were salutary. In her letter of 30 May 1984, announcing their plans to return to Trivandrum on 1 June, Kamala Das buoyantly writes: 'Glowing with health, a surprise gift from the Lankan Gods whoever they are.'[32] Apparently, in July, she had an 'encouraging' meeting with Mrs Indira Gandhi in Trivandrum. Her eldest son, M.D. Nalapat, recalls: 'I was in an anteroom when the meeting took place, but Amma was very happy afterwards and spoke warmly about Mrs G and believed that the feeling was mutual.'[33] Apparently,

Kamala Das recorded her impressions in 'The First Meeting': her apprehension and vulnerability, as well as the unexpected 'fragile comeliness' behind the leader's poster persona as 'a giantess of myriad / Destinies . . . who wore on her face / the features of an entire land.'[34] On 31 October Mrs Indira Gandhi was assassinated and there were anti-Sikh riots in Delhi. In 'Delhi-1984' Kamala Das visits that 'terror, fleet of foot, [which] did rampage / the sedate suburbs, while in the queen's / funeral pyre the embers lay cooling.'

When new elections were held in November–December 1984, to many of us, Kamala Das's decision to contest as an independent candidate from Kerala came as a surprise. It was probably a combination of several factors that had led her to take that decision. Her experience of the ethnic conflict in Sri Lanka, her meeting with Mrs Gandhi earlier in July, the anti-Sikh riots, and her sense of growing religious tensions in her home state had ignited her commitment to the social causes of women and children and of promoting religious harmony. And thus was born her grand ambition to 'help to rid my homeland of religious animosities' and 'write a poem to end all poems, a poem absolute as the tomb'.[35] However, she had neither the stamina nor the money to cope with the nitty-gritty of politics, so she lost, with only 1780 friendly votes of the two hundred thousand or more that she had expected and needed. She forayed into electoral politics once more in 2000 when, shortly after her conversion to Islam, she attempted to set up the Lok Seva Party to promote secularism and provide asylum to orphaned mothers.[36] These experiences only led her to rediscover that active politics for her was a slippery path.

After her return from Sri Lanka, her *Collected Poems* vol. I was published by the Navakerala Printers, Trivandrum, and she sent me a copy. The book had virtually gone unnoticed but for the report that appeared in October 1984 in several Indian newspapers that Kamala Das was a nominee for the Nobel Prize for Literature. The prize for that year went to the Czech poet Jaroslav Seifert, but Kamala Das, feeling honoured by the reported nomination, responded in a newspaper interview and said, 'I feel like P.T. Usha.'[37] It saddened her when Khushwant Singh spiced up his gossipy weekly column 'With Malice towards One and All' with the canard that Kamala Das had herself planted the story in the press. She promptly refuted his allegation in a letter to the editor in the *Hindustan Times*, 3 November 1984:

> I was sad to read the lie circulated by Khushwant Singh in the 'Malice' column (HT, Oct. 20). He was trying to make your readers believe that by [sic] Nobel Prize candidature was only a canard floated by me . . . When Yasumari Kawabata . . . received the Nobel Prize for Literature KS wrote against him in the *Illustrated Weekly of India*. KS apparently likes only hack writers.
>
> The latest copy of *Artes*, the Journal of the Royal Swedish Academy, carried several poems of mine and an excerpt from my much maligned autobiography. The translator is Mr Östen Sjöstrand, Member of the Nobel Committee. What KS and other Indian columnists dislike are admired by members of the Nobel Committee.

Since Khushwant Singh did not respond to her rebuttal and since his allegation in reference to Kamala Das resurfaced in *Outlook* magazine 2003 in a tongue-in-cheek 'investigative' piece on various Indian 'aspirants' and 'perspirants' angling for the Nobel Prize,[38] a comment or two here may not be out of place to clear the mist.

While it is true that the details of the four-phase process of selection for the Nobel Prize remain confidential for fifty years, and a complete picture is not yet available, certain facts need to be taken into account. The first list of around two hundred candidates is compiled from an even larger list of nominations received annually by invitation from over six hundred academics and literary and cultural organizations worldwide: this means that some of the proposed names may continue to be mentioned even after the initial two-hundred-odd names are pruned down by April to some twenty or so names. This list is further reduced to about five names by mid-September before a final decision is reached in October.

Evidently, there had been some interest in Kamala Das's work in the Swedish Academy since translations of an extract from *My Story* and six of her poems, viz. 'A Hot Noon in Malabar', 'Radha Krishna', 'Visitors to the City', 'Composition', 'The Inheritance', and 'An Introduction' appeared in the Swedish bimonthly magazine *Artes* in 1984, in the July–August issue.[39] Östen Sjöstrand, the Swedish poet and translator and founder-editor of the magazine, was also a member of the Swedish Academy which is involved in processing nominations for the Nobel Prize in Literature. According to the Swedish critic Curt Bladh, when Östen Sjöstrand became a member of the Swedish Academy in 1975, the year he founded *Artes*, he gained 'insight into the discussions preceding the Nobel Prize in Literature and several prize winners were previously featured in *Artes*'. In order to stimulate the process of selection, samples from the works of other writers, for example, the Czech poet Jaroslav Seifert, winner of the prize in 1984, appeared in the September–October issue of 1984. It needs to be noted that Kamala Das's poems appeared in the July–August 1984 issue when the decision-making process was at the second and third stages.

*

Although Kamala Das was disappointed over losing the parliamentary elections she stood for, her loss in her political career was to be her gain in poetry. Exhausted by the election campaign, she retired to recuperate in her sister's home in the Anamalai Hills in Tamil Nadu. Here in January 1985, she wrote the Anamalai sequence of fifteen short poems. As the critic P.P. Raveendran has noted, she channelled 'the troubled psyche of a writer' by celebrating 'the self in the tradition of the classical Tamil *akam* ("interior") poems, without recourse to the more familiar "confessional" trope of her poetry'.[40]

In 1985, Kamala Das won the Sahitya Akademi Award in English for *Collected Poems* vol. I. In her acceptance speech at the Writers Meet on 25 February 1986, instead of offering the customary thanks, Kamala took the opportunity to upbraid the Akademi, though with informed humour, for concentrating overmuch on the old classics and bestowing awards and citations on writers only when 'their fecundity is exhausted'. It would be better to provide them, especially women writers like her, with opportunities through resident fellowships for creative solitude undistracted by financial and familial anxieties. Comparing the writing of a book to the experience of childbearing, Kamala Das urged the Akademi to 'act as a midwife to coax out creations from contemporary writers'.

As it happened, 1986 was also the year of international travel for Kamala Das. She was invited to participate in the Adelaide Festival of Arts, Writers' Week, in March 1986. To coincide with her visit, the Centre for Research in the New Literatures in English, University of Adelaide, brought out *Kamala Das: A Selection with Essays on Her Work*, edited by S.C. Harrex and Vincent O'Sullivan, the distinguished New Zealand poet. In October later in the year, she was among the group of Indian writers selected to represent India at the Frankfurt Book Fair where India was the guest of honour that year. Kamala Das remained productive. She sent me new poems—'The Return of Hitler', 'The New Sinhala Films', 'Hairpins and Rubber-Bands'—as well as the experimental, unpunctuated short story 'running away from home' which appeared in 1985 and 1986 in the revived *Indian Literary Review* which I co-edited with Suresh Kohli. In 1991 *Best of Kamala Das*, edited by P.P. Raveendran, was published. It included the Sri Lanka poems as well as ten poems of the Anamalai sequence.

In the summer of 1992, Kamala Das lost her husband who had been ailing for some time. In her letter of 2 December 1992, from Trivandrum, she described how she was coping with her loss, her loneliness and her reduced vision:

> After Das has left, this house and all have begun to look oddly unfamiliar. Strange voices wake me up at midnight and make obscene suggestions. I have lost all my desire for survival . . . I cannot read much. My right eye seems to have gone blind. Cried myself blind, I guess. I went to Jamaica after D's death and read out a few poems. Talked of feminism too. Stunned the unsuspecting audience . . . I am actually having a bad time, loneliness and all but I do not let others see it. Tried to write poems in English but they disappointed me . . . I am bored here, seated glum in the drawing room receiving messages of condolences nearly four months after D's departure.

Soon after, she moved to live in Cochin to be closer to her third son, Jaisurya. As a way of coping with her emotional difficulties, she turned, or rather returned, to painting, as she had done earlier in the 1980s, an art form that she had enjoyed since her schooldays. Now she took up painting female nudes as an extension of, or even as a temporary substitute for, her poetry. By gleefully announcing that 'I find the nude female body the most beautiful in the world', she seemed to enjoy the risk of shocking her 'respectable' Malayali audience once again. In October 1994 she held her first-ever art exhibition, appropriately titled 'The Unfinished Women'. Clearly pleased with it, she declared to me a month before travelling to London and coming to Germany, where I lived, that 'Life seems new.'

Her reading in London was supported by Antonia Byatt, then head of literature, the Southbank Centre, and her visit to Germany (6–19 November) followed. She arrived at Düsseldorf Airport on a wheelchair and made her way with effort to the attic flat my wife and I lived in on the fourth floor. The visit was a very precious period for us all; slowly, the obvious traces of mourning she wore receded. She told us about how she had abandoned all will to survive after her husband's death, and had virtually starved herself for days till she had to be hospitalized. The conversations turned to life in Germany, and all things German. She explored various types of seeded bread, and spent a considerable amount of time buying gifts for various members of her family. She joked, interacted and drew a portrait of a nun jointly with our then six-year-old daughter.

Her readings were well received, and she herself was in good spirits despite her chronic problems of health and the cold weather, and had animated interactions with my colleagues. 'I had a marvellous time . . . and a sense of security,' she wrote, and remembered how much she had relished the German cheeses and other delicacies, and of course Sekt—the German equivalent of champagne—that always brought a smile to her face.

For some time after her husband's death, Kamala Das was not happy with the poems she was able to write and, whether out of despair or perhaps to give undistracted time to her poetry, she had also withdrawn from writing newspaper columns. But, in her letter of 27 March 1995, she had regained her confidence: 'I am once again busy with my columns and poetry editorship.' And to get away from 'badgering' visitors, she was planning to move away from Cochin. In the same letter she also mentions visits from 'a Canadian writer Merrily Weisbord [who] has been here for the past few days following me about with a tape recorder,' wanting her to visit Canada and collaborate with her on writing a book on feminism.

This reference to feminism would be surprising to anyone who has read Kamala Das's work or followed her life closely; they would recognize that she had never been emotionally inclined or ideologically committed to be defined by the politics of feminism: for her, except in biological terms, there was hardly any difference between a man and a woman. As she put it in her letter of 22 July 1995:

> The Canadian publishers have sent me a Dictaphone & tapes. I have yet to operate it. Feminism tastes like soggy cardboard. I am bored with it all. I wish I could eat cyanide & die. Looking around for a way out.

However, the visits from Merrily Weisbord were the beginning of a new and welcome acquaintance which culminated in Weisbord's 'memoir of a friendship', published in 2010, a year after the poet's death.

Clearly, Kamala had regained her buoyancy, as in the same letter she spoke enthusiastically of inaugurating the new Lawrence Durrell Centre at St Berchmans' College, Changanassery, on 21 July 1995; this would be 'bringing Durrell's ashes home'. Kamala was also excited about a forthcoming lecture trip to the US and Canada with Merrily Weisbord.

With increased opportunities for international travel and cultural participation, Kamala Das's renewed confidence was visible in a new selection of her poems, *Only the Soul Knows How to Sing*, published in 1996 with a sensitive introduction by the poet and critic K. Satchidanandan. The volume included several new poems on familiar themes, 'A Widow's Lament', 'A Faded Epaulet on His Shoulder', as well as others inspired by her Canadian sojourn such as 'A Feminist's Lament' and 'Ode to Quebec'.

When Jaisurya was transferred to Pune in 1997, Kamala felt herself 'without a guardian', as it were, and found it 'depressing'. Despite a successful eye surgery in Chennai she had 'turned half blind', returned to art and wrote only one column. She moved to a quieter locality in Cochin. The new place had a guest suite adjacent to it that could also serve as her art studio when she did not have guests staying with her. Writing on 29 November 1997, she seemed pleased with exchanges with her visiting friends and house guests:

> The present guest is a BBC girl who is also a travel writer. Last month a Canadian critic named James Brigham stayed here for a week. He heads a Lawrence Durrell Centre in Canada . . . I dream of the three of you visiting Cochin & staying with me.

And yet, this seems to have been a poetically lean and emotionally lonely period for her. The three poems which she published in 1998 in *Kavya Bharati* focus on the sense of redundancy felt by widows at the temple ghats in Kashi, 'beggared by their loved ones' death', or by old mothers who in their own homes are seen to 'stain' the dreams of their sons and 'cause errors in the computers of their lives'. In the third poem, it is the poet who is 'a mute remnant of what I was': having misplaced the divining rod, she feels 'beggared' by its loss like 'the withering of a limb / with blinded eyes'.

Unfortunately, we did not manage to visit her then as we had wished to. But a year later, at sixty-five, Kamala Das underwent another phase of reinvention. She was courted by and fell in love with a Muslim scholar and announced her conversion to Islam on 16 December 1999. Although the reasons for conversion were private, calling a press conference to announce it gave it a polemical dimension, bringing together the wrath of both fundamentalists and feminists, though for different reasons. Commenting on her conversion, the editorial of an Indian newspaper dwelt on the uneasy contradictions in Kamala Das, citing 'I am a freak' from an early poem of hers. In her more balanced assessment, 'The Freedom and Bondage of Madhavikutty', Leela Menon dwelt on the complex issues involved. Religion and conversion being a private choice, it was irrelevant whether the conversion was 'spiritually inspired or matrimonially motivated'. With Kamala Das being an icon of the postcolonial woman who could also be an iconoclast, there would have been a public reaction to her conversion even if she had not called a press conference to announce it.

However, some of her pronouncements had a polarizing effect, the lauding of the burqa, for example. Kamala Das did not do anything half-heartedly. From celebrating the freedom of 'the dancing shoe' to publicly embracing the secure anonymity of the burqa was certainly a provocative leap. But, given her capacity for reinventing herself, the trajectory from Amy, Madhavikutty, Kamala Das, Radha/Meera in spirit to Kamala Suraiya does not seem illogical after all. Nor does it seem inconsistent, given its context of a newfound love, with Kamala Das's view of poetry as an art originating in the experience of love, human and divine.

On 17 December 2003, four years after her conversion, using a thick red marker pen, Kamala wrote:

Enclosing faded poetry . . . Typists are Literature MAs but make mistakes[.] I am almost blind. Otherwise I would write when I remember you and Vijaya and the little fraulein. Send me a recent photograph. Sending mine—Not particularly unhappy. Not happy either.

Both 'Faded Poetry', a sequence of four poems, and the short poem below are suggestive of the grey mood of stocktaking by one who never ceased to reinvent, and in the process, contradict herself:

I wore a mock wedding ring
for these past few years
imagined myself
a married woman
ultimately,
life crowds you out
and truth strangles
the reality of your mind;
in the final analysis
made by sepulchral
history
He would become
a good father
and I,
a competent poet,
nothing else . . .

With the same letter Kamala Das also enclosed the brochure of *Orientations* ('When I dance, I am a woman'), an intercultural play staged in England by Border Crossings in October 2003. Interweaving 'myth and present day narrative to tell a tale of gender and sexuality in present day India', the play incorporated 'The Doubt' by Kamala Das which, in a 'dialogue of one', wonders at the underlying androgyny in questions that relate to differentiation between the male and female, body and soul. With its unsentimental tone, conversational manner, its extension of the theme through argument and visual imagery, and crisp diction, serious and playful at the same time, the poem is reminiscent of John Donne's 'The Ecstasy'.

In subsequent years, owing to Kamala Das's failing eyesight, we had limited correspondence but we often conversed on the phone, as in 2004, when I was invited to update my entry on Kamala Das for the *Routledge Encyclopaedia of Post-colonial Literatures* (2005). The following year, when my colleague and co-editor Barbara Schmidt-Haberkamp and I decided to include Kamala Das's short story 'Summer Vacation' in *Contemporary Indian Short Stories*,[41] she surprised us with a new version, translated by herself.

In the summer of 2006 when I was in Delhi, Kamala telephoned and asked me to go meet her. M.D. Nalapat, her eldest son, had also flown in from Delhi. The visit (6–9 August), the last time I saw her, was filled with conversations, touching on several incidents, past and more recent in her life, on relationships, friends and family, and the contours of her friendship with Merrily Weisbord and her growing serious reservations about the direction and the perspective on Kamala that Weisbord wanted to give to her book, which was no longer a collaboration on feminism. I wrote down some of what she said in my diary notes. Sadly, after she moved to Pune, we could not meet, owing to restrictions placed then on my own travel by illness. But we stayed in contact by telephone and by email messages conveyed through Jaisurya. 'The bond . . . that exists between us shall go on,' she had said in her letter of 26 February 1982, and that indeed proved to be the case. Unable to see clearly and write, in her last note of 31 July 2008 from Pune, using a thick black marker pen, she announced: 'Arthritis has stopped my writing. A new spirit has come to live in my body.' We spoke on the phone a few times during the months before she died on 31 May 2009 and I had the impression that she was aware that the end was nearing.

'I speak three languages, write in two, dream in one'

Kamala Das was certainly an unconventional combination of a poet in English and a fiction writer in Malayalam. While her poetic self was shaped by her long years in the cosmopolitan English-speaking coastal cities of Calcutta and Bombay, its springs lay in her childhood reared in her ancestral Malabar landscape. Madhavikutty, who enthralled and provoked her Malayalam readers with her short stories, drew inspiration from the way the line between truth and fiction would often dissolve when she was regaled with anecdotes and the local gossip by the servants in Nalapat House. 'The voices of these storytellers' and their tales resurfaced in her imagination when, on the advice of her psychiatrist friend Dr Ramanlal Patel in the 1960s and 1970s, she began to recall her childhood memories; these further triggered her imagination and filtered into the short stories and poems she wrote. Her two selves, the poet and the storyteller, complemented each other, although she was quintessentially a poet, unwaveringly true to the line: 'I write in two [languages], dream in one,' the instinctive language of imagination. 'Which untaught language / do I speak in my dreams . . . ?' she asks rhetorically in 'The River Saraswati' and lets the poem be the answer. Only once, I think, when pressed in an interview in 1993, she responded: 'I dream in English, I am afraid.'[42]

Indeed, her short stories in English and in English translation are strikingly poetic in content and structure, and some of them read like a dream sequence—for example, 'On the Mountain Slopes' or 'running away from home', in which the unpunctuated, breathless narrative enacts Minnie's stream of consciousness and incorporates, as a kind of mini-autobiography, some of the aspects that figure in *My Story*.[43] Unsurprisingly, K. Satchidanandan finds her stories 'at times . . . pure poetry, just emotional contexts with no narrative content'.[44] She affirmed this when she remarked: 'I see poetry in an experience, and then see good prose coming out of the same experience.'[45]

In fact, not only the ferment for her autobiography, *My Story*, but also the poetic underpinning of its ostensibly linear but rather episodic narrative can be traced to the poem that she had published in 1950s in the *Indian PEN* magazine. Exactly in the middle of *My Story* in chapter 25, titled 'The Blood-stained Moonlight' in the first edition and 'A Desire to Die' in subsequent editions, we have the troubled narrator leaving her sleeping family, climbing up to her terrace. Gazing down she sees puddles of moonlight in the courtyard and on the dark winding road leading up to a fishing colony:

> I wanted for a moment, to fling myself down, to spatter the blanched brilliance of the moonlight with red blood stains. The moon moved in haste as though it had a date to keep. Under the lamp-post a mad beggar was doing a solo dance lifting his emaciated hands in the air and muttering to himself. The rhythm of his grotesque dance seized my legs. My hair fell loose around my face. I felt then that I was dancing on the most desolate pinnacle of the world. The dance of the last human being (p. 104)

Returning to her room in a 'somnambulist' state, she writes a poem that speaks of a resolve to 'Wipe out the paints, unmould the clay. / Let nothing remain of that yesterday', to write about 'a new life' wherein her grief and pain would float over as poems 'darkly as heavy monsoon clouds do in the sky'.

My Story owes much, therefore, to Kamala Das's poetic instinct. Many ideas, images and even lines from her poems can be found in the autobiography; likewise, her poems are imbued with images from her own life. Two of her longer poems, 'Composition' and 'The Suicide', have much in common with the tenor and setting of *My Story*, although they were written and published earlier. For example, the penultimate chapter of *My Story* ('Who were we to sit beside their favourite God?' changed to 'A Freedom to Dis-Compose') not only expatiates on but incorporates the last thirty-odd lines of 'Composition', concluding with 'I must linger on, / trapped in immortality, / my only freedom being / the freedom to / discompose'. The Malayalam version, *Ente Katha*, was serialized two years before the English one; however, going by textual evidence, Kamala Das had started writing her story even before she was commissioned to; she was in hospital when she was approached by the publisher of *Malayalnadu* for its serialization. V.B.C. Nair, the editor of *Malayalnadu*, has on record acknowledged that the first chapter of *Ente Katha* was translated from the original in English by Kakkanadan.

This may be clever genre-crossing but there is evidence to suggest that Kamala Das had intended or begun to find a poetic form for what eventually became *Ente Katha*/*My Story*. In the Malayalam version, instead of the one-page preface to *My Story*, there is a six-page preface entitled 'A Sparrow's Sorrow', in the version translated by Meena Pillai. Significantly, the same preface in Kamala Das's original English version, entitled 'The Sparrow on the Glass-Pane', was published in *Dialogue*.[46] In the opening lines, the writer recalls the sight of a sparrow flying through the ventilator of her room, hitting its breast against the fan and, though wounded and bleeding, still flying towards the window and getting stuck to the glass. The act of writing what subsequently becomes her 'autobiography' is then like bleeding on to paper and, through dying, becoming a poem. That it settled into the form of prose rather than the more fluid form of poetry she attributes to her lack of artistic maturity:

> I call this a poem although after creating a beautiful turbulence inside me the words shed their music as they surface and settle into the steadier pattern of prose. I was always hoping to be able to write this. But a poem does not ripen for you, you have to ripen for it.

An autobiographer is both the subject matter and the structural centre of whatever she is writing. Even when she is consciously or subconsciously selecting or modifying what she thinks must go into the text, the author believes that whatever she is writing is either true or should be regarded as being true by the reader. The voice of the autobiographer is intimate or familiar, unlike that of the biographer, even though it may focus more on external events and her/his public persona—as, for example, in the case of Jawaharlal Nehru's autobiography, 'this egotistical narrative of my adventures through life, such as they are . . . up to 1935', with only passing references to his wife: 'I almost overlooked her.'[47] The point of view is almost always in the first person, although Gertrude Stein's *The Autobiography of Alice Toklas* and more recently Salman Rushdie's *Joseph Anton* are exceptions. The reader too expects or likes to believe that the autobiographer is telling the truth, even if the account is not immediately verifiable in a factual sense.

There is however a basic difference between a woman's autobiography and a man's autobiography. Wayne Shumaker characterizes 'the typical [man's] autobiography as a summing up, a review of the whole life or an important segment of it—the stepping back of a painter to have a look at the finished canvas.'[48] In contrast to the tightly organized autobiographies of men, women's autobiographies have a loose structure and 'are more like diaries, honest records of the moment, white-hot, which do not "impose the order of the next day on the record of the previous day."'[49] What Virginia Woolf said of her *Diary* is true in varying degrees of many other women's autobiographies as well, including *My Story*: 'Something loose knit and yet not slovenly, so elastic that it will embrace anything, solemn, slight or beautiful that comes into my mind.'

Truth or Lie: The 'Perjur'd I/Eye'

Unlike autobiography, poetry is not assumed or *expected* to be factually true even when it draws on the real events in the poet's life. Poetry channels into words a complex of emotions and ideas aroused by real and imagined events. Unlike an autobiography, which provides the space to annotate or expand, in a poem ideas are compressed so as to cohere in images and rhythm that derive their fluidity from association and parallelism.

The conflict between poetry and truth is as old as Plato who banned poets from his Republic for being liars, for not telling the truth as it is defined in philosophical terms. The pleasure that poetry gives us arises partly from the way it constructs and interprets the actual events; this process involves an element of fiction, exaggeration or, to quote Shakespeare, 'perjury'. While professing his love to the Dark Lady on oath, Shakespeare admits in the same sonnet: 'For I have sworn thee fair; more perjur'd eye, / To swear against the truth so foul a lie!' In asserting that his beloved is beautiful, he admits that his eye or he himself is doubly a liar for telling a lie after promising to tell the truth. The advice to the poet, in a poem by Robert Graves, is that 'Nice contradiction between fact and fact / Will make the whole read human and exact.' 'Tell all the truth,' urged Emily Dickinson, 'but tell it slant—'. This explains why even in a 'confessional' poem such as Sylvia Plath's 'Daddy', while the speaker attempts to liberate herself from repressive patriarchal images by metaphorically killing her father, she 'constructs' him into a Nazi whereas Plath's real father was not a Nazi, and her mother was not Jewish. In a similar vein, in one of her poems Kamala Das portrays her autocratic father as the person whom she feared the most, only 'next to Indira Gandhi', and in yet another poem as 'the most important man to die in Calicut / Since Vasco trod the sands at Kappad'. Given that Kamala Das's method of construction in *My Story* was by intention and design towards achieving a poetic form—even as a lucrative commission for its serialization accelerated the pace of writing—the question of how much of *My Story* is factual or fictional, though enticing, needs to be viewed in its intertextual relation to her poetry. As for the element of invention/reinvention, in her autobiography or in her poetry, she acknowledged the role of the 'perjured eye / I' on the question of infidelity or adultery, whether acted in body or enacted in the mind:

> I'll not swear everything in that book [*My Story*] happened to me. I exaggerated a little bit. You may not have had sex but it figured in the thoughts. If there was an opportunity, who knows? If it's red, make it redder. It's the artist's freedom to deepen the colour.[50]

Influences: Family and Literary

Kamala Das discovered the freedom to write in her childhood and adolescence at Nalapat, her ancestral home in Malabar where she spent long summer vacations and on one occasion a whole year away from Calcutta. That was also the period when she made the literary discoveries that shaped her poetic sensibility and her world view. Growing up in two different parts of India, she experienced a sense of multiple dislocations that were emotional, linguistic, cultural and geographic. That could well explain the contradictions in her poetic persona and in her pronouncements about her life and her work that bewilder many a reader and critic.

There were contrasting lifestyles which she had to cope with: colonial, urban, cosmopolitan, in English- and Bengali-speaking Calcutta, and the rural, idyllic, nationalist, in Malayalam-speaking Malabar. In Calcutta, the very brown girl felt discriminated against in a Catholic school and lonely at home, with 'a vague and indifferent' poet-mother and a discipline-enforcing father who imposed the Gandhian model of austerity. At the sprawling Nalapat House there was a joint family with a demonstratively affectionate grandmother, the reclusive great-grandmother and her sister, and her intellectually engaging grand-uncle, besides servants entertaining her with stories and local gossip and a variety of people coming and going. In the restricted home in Calcutta, desperate for company, Kamala would call out to the hawkers to interact with them as she loved listening to their stories. Both in Calcutta and Nalapat, talking about sex was a taboo, and her dark complexion was seen as exceptional ('I was the first dark girl in the family'). While at the convent in Calcutta sin was recurrently invoked, at Nalapat there were family stories about early marriage, sacrificing wives at odds with the lost and remembered matriarchal lineage. Disenchanted with the austerity of her parents and her grandmother, wearing white homespun khadi, Kamala was charmed, instead, by the second wife of her grand-uncle, 'my favourite aunt', who always wore jewellery and perfume, even as she 'walked up every night the steep staircase of the gatehouse to meet her famous husband in their lush bedroom, kept fragrant with incense and jasmine garlands'. Returning to Nalapat after her eleventh birthday and listening to the thudding of the drums at the Para festival, the roar of the *velichappadu* as he became possessed, and the songs of the Parayankaali dancers, the English- and Bengali-speaking Kamala who had been raised in Calcutta 'turned into a girl who was part of a dream, the mute princess of the fairy tale'.[51]

In contrast to the stiff school-textbook-driven schedule in Calcutta, Nalapat offered the freedom to innovate. She staged, with her brother, Malayalam adaptations of Victor Hugo's *Les Misérables*, Kalidas's *Sakuntalam*, and played Eponine, Hugo's tragic heroine who dies for her unrequited love of Marius, and Nur Jahan, the cultured, charismatic and commanding Mughal queen. When Kamala Das reached puberty and learnt that she was biologically capable of being a mother, she began to dream of marriage and children. Inspired by the story of Kunti, the mother of the Pandavas, Kamala Das bared her body to the sun, offering herself, and prayed for a son but 'no God came forward to claim me as his woman'. She used to hang a picture of Lord Byron 'with a black cape over his shoulders and thick, wavy hair' on her bedroom wall so that she would not miss it when she woke up in the morning; so attached was she to the picture that her grandmother's fear that she might marry a Christian could not be set to rest even though Kamala assured her that he was dead.

In Calcutta, translations of the national writers Rabindranath Tagore, Sarat Chandra and Bankim Chandra engaged her with 'their moody essence' but at Nalapat she had the opportunity to explore the uncharted in her grand-uncle's library of European and classical Indian literature. Brought up on stories from the Indian classics and the mythological love of Radha and Krishna that she heard from her grandmother, it was through her precocious reading of Oscar Wilde, Turgenev, Anatole France, Flaubert's *Madame Bovary*, Tolstoy's *Anna Karenina*, Abbé Prévost's *Manon Lescaut* and Walt Whitman's *Leaves of Grass* that she 'ripened fast on adult diet'. Reminding her of her three distinct cultures—Malabari, Bengali and English—her grand-uncle taught her to value the importance of nurturing her individuality; in contrast, her teachers in Calcutta advised her 'to merge with the crowd'. Her mathematics teacher even admonished her: 'Kamala, why do you take delight in always doing something different? Can't you behave like everyone else? Do you want to make yourself conspicuous?'[52]

Another contradiction that the young Kamala faced was that, though she was born into the matrilineal tradition, both her grandmother, whose affection she cherished, and her poet-mother seemed to her to have compromised with patriarchal values. There is no doubt that Kamala Das emulated her mother who could afford to keep herself free of household chores in order to write poetry, but, unlike her mother, she had to wait, at least during the early years of her married life, till the family was asleep before she could use the kitchen table as her desk for writing. She also emulated Ammalu Amma, her great-grandmother's younger sister, who would engrave her verses with a stylus on stiff palmyra leaves. In 'The Palmyra Tree'[53], one of her last poems, as Kamala Das mourns the cutting of the ancient tree in the decaying, 'ungainly' Nalapat house, she also remembers 'the loud flapping of the Palmyra leaves and the sound of bones cracking' which she had heard when she was growing up in Malabar. It is probably this 'ancestral' voice that she refers to in one of the verse lines she had inscribed in 1978 in my copy of *The Old Playhouse and Other Poems* when she had asked, 'Devendra, have you heard the vultures cough / like grandfathers from the palmyra boughs?' However, she did not find her mother's work empowering because Balamani Amma 'never wrote freely, frankly', and confined herself to 'God and domestic bliss', the prescribed themes for women's writing, while ignoring 'the body, the physicality'.

Historically, among Kamala Das's poetic ancestors are the Buddhist nuns of the sixth century BC who in some of their songs in *Therigatha* celebrate freedom from marriage and the drudgery of a housewife, and Muddupalani, a scholarly courtesan/devadasi in the Thanjavur court, whose eighteenth-century Telugu erotic recasting of the story of Radha and Krishna in *Radhika Santwanam* (The Appeasing of Radhika) was banned in 1887.[54] Although Muddupalani's epic poem was reprinted in 1911, and *Psalms of the Sisters* (translated by C.A.F. Rhys-Davids) and *Poems of Indian Women* (selected by Margaret Macnicol) were published in 1909 and 1923 respectively, it was not until 1991 that *Women's Writing in India: 600 B.C. to the Present* (edited by Susie Tharu and K. Lalita) brought the extant texts from Indian women's poetry into limelight. There is no evidence to suggest that Kamala Das had read any of these. As late as 1986 she lamented that when she was growing up there was no tradition to fall back on, no model to emulate:

> We had Avvayyar [the Tamil Sangam poets], Meerabai, but they wrote of God, they sang of God. That was allowed. But what happens to you, what happens to a woman, when a man becomes her god, her living god? Has she no right to write about that god?[55]

There in a nutshell we have the yet unformulated love-ethic of Kamala Das: looking for the divine in her man or for the man in the divine. Such a romantic view of love is, paradoxically, both liberating and confining. It rewrites the chemistry of love: it resents imposed bondage but it rejoices being spontaneously in thrall.

It is ironic that at age fifteen when her life of imagination was being nurtured by notions of individuality and romantic love, in real life Kamala Das was married off to someone not of her choice. In fact, as Kamala Das tells us, it was partly her poor performance in mathematics and partly her apparently unconventional behaviour and ebullience that seems to have been a factor in her father arranging an early marriage. It appears to be the case that, given the prevailing social and economic structure, her father did what most middle-class parents would do, acting on the firm but possibly erroneous belief that what they were doing was in the best interest of their daughter.

Kamala speaks of this unintentional irony—the discrepancy between what parents want for their children, and what the children themselves might seek—with gentle directness when she describes the arranged marriage as being sent on a family mission:

> I was sent away to protect my family's
> Honour, to save a few cowards, to defend some
> Abstractions, sent to another city to be
> A relative's wife . . .[56]

Although Kamala Das did not approve of her arranged match, she had, as she reminded her sister Sulochana Nalapat in her letter of 26 July 1958, given in to parental wishes without outward fuss:

> I was persuaded to marry, and I had no courage to refuse to do what even my father wanted me to do. I have not shown by a word or sign that I felt trapped. Let down and disillusioned.[57]

The sense of being trapped and of victimhood implied here, however, became a recurrent theme in her poetry. When an arranged marriage which she had embraced out of filial loyalty failed to measure up to her love-ethic, she needed and created the poetic *persona* of the rebellious daughter: 'All the commandments engraved on the columns of my mind gradually faded, the fierce winds rising out of the Ganges devoured their words and I changed into a disobedient daughter.'[58] In retrospect, Kamala Das traced this transforming spirit of self-reinvention to the 'adult diet' of books that she had fed on in her adolescence:

> Ask the books that I read why I changed. Ask the authors dead and alive who communicated with me and gave me the courage to be myself. The books like a mother-cow licked the calf of my thought into shape and left me to lie at the altar of the world as a sacrificial gift.[59]

Of the various 'adult' books that she read in Malabar, perhaps the ones that had the most important influences on her thinking and her poetry were Abbé Prévost's *Manon Lescaut* and Walt Whitman's *Leaves of Grass*. Seven months before she fell in love with a Muslim and converted to Islam and ten years before she died, Kamala Das declared Abbé Prévost's *Manon Lescaut* to have been 'the only book that's touched me to the marrow'. She said it

> let me into the magical secrets of love. For months I walked in a daze searching for my lover. Did that book wound my life? Did it take me far away from reality? I don't know for certain, I was unmoulded and reshaped by Provost.[60]

Set in early-eighteenth-century Paris, *Manon Lescaut* is a story of an aristocratic young man, Chevalier des Grieux, who falls in love at first sight with Manon Lescaut, a young woman of humble birth, who is reluctantly being sent to a convent by her father. Manon persuades des Grieux to elope but financial exigencies complicate

Manon de Lescaut, Kamala Das. 2005. Taken from Kamala Das, *Poetic Sketches*, in *Encountering Kamala: Selections from the Poetry of Kamala Das*, with an Introduction by Andrew Arkin (New York: Gorgeous Notions Press, 2007).

their plans. Despite loving des Grieux to distraction, she is 'fickle and flighty', wondering whether 'fidelity is a foolish virtue . . . when one is short of bread?' Des Grieux and Manon's life of passion and pursuit undergoes various vicissitudes, including betrayal and reunion, thieving, prison and deportation, ending in her tragic death in the wilderness of New Orleans. An anonymous narrator tells the story in reported speech the way des Grieux had told him in retrospection. This narrative mode raises the question of how reliable the version is and whether Manon was 'a thief and a whore, the image of love itself, or a thoroughly modern woman'. In the absence of direct speech, Manon's character remains ambiguous but powerful enough to enthral des Grieux and in the process challenge the patriarchal and class politics of the time.

The novel, written when the author was in exile in Holland, was banned in Paris; it draws on Abbé Prévost's own tragic love affairs, his conflict with his father and with his Benedictine order, his conversion to the Anglican church, and his subsequent pardon for his apostasy by the Pope and reconciliation with the Roman Catholic Church. At the centre of the novel *Manon Lescaut*, couched in the poetic and religious language of devotion, is the notion of plenitudinous secular love and the suffering that surrendering oneself to it brings. However, implicit in this complex story of the spiritual possibilities of love is also the alternative of transcending the secular through devotional love as exemplified by the Bhakti poets who rebelled against the socially and politically prescribed and controlled religion of the time.

Arvind Krishna Mehrotra explains the love-ethic of Meera's own devotional poems in his annotation of 'Meera', a poem by Arun Kolatkar:

> Hers are songs of praise and rapture, of supplication and distress, but of rebellion as well. Meera overturned the normative values

of Hinduism and the conventions of a patriarchal society to celebrate an uninhibited devotion to her god-lover (Krishna) rather than fidelity to her legitimate husband.[61]

While Kamala Das's affinities to Meera's love-ethic are apparent, what she felt was lacking in Meera's 'uninhibited' celebration of her sublimated love was, as mentioned earlier, 'the body, the physicality', the here and now: 'What happens to a woman, when a man becomes her god, her living god? Has she no right to write about that god?' If this suggests that Kamala Das's love-ethic was stuck in the patriarchal groove of two unequal humans in which the woman deifies the man, it needs to be remembered that in *Manon Lescaut*, the book that touched her deeply, it is an aristocratic young man des Grieux who risks everything for his love of the socially inferior Manon.

The second book to have a lasting influence on Kamala Das was Walt Whitman's *Leaves of Grass*. At first sight, the poet's bearded face on the frontispiece reminded her of 'the Christian God in my schoolbook of catechism who stood behind some clouds gesturing angrily to Adam and Eve to get out of the Garden of Eden'[62] but as she began to read his poems,[63] she found Whitman both liberal and liberating:

> I went into his poetry as one enters a new continent, with expectation and always a little out of breath . . . When he talked of the forenoon purple of the hills I looked out of the grill and saw my green estate, my palms, my mango trees and the deeper green that hid the sea from me . . . I looked at the tall trees that brought forth their fragrant blossoms in spring and began to worry about their death . . . I felt at times that the poet from the far-off country was looking down with hypnotic eyes from the sky above our red-tiled house.

Consider you who peruse me whether
I may not in unknown ways be looking upon you
You furnish your parts toward eternity
Great or small, you furnish your parts toward the soul.

Whitman, she felt, invited her to recognize her own self, in body and in soul, free of an inhibiting sense of hierarchy. In contrast to the stories of silently suffering women she had heard about in her family, Whitman struck a revolutionary chord, declaring 'I am the poet of the woman the same as the man, / And I say it is as great to be a woman as to be a man, / And I say there is nothing greater than the mother of men.' Whitman's egalitarianism, his empathy for the black, the poor and underprivileged, and his rejection of social and political hierarchy stuck Kamala Das who was always uncomfortable with caste and class divisions. It was Whitman's 'wide sweep', like that of life in Nature, embracing all, contradicting himself yet 'humbled' by 'the growing knowledge of the world' that appealed to her open-hearted curiosity. In the current climate of feminist revisionism of social and literary history, and in view of her affinity to Indian women devotional poets, Kamala Das's self-discovery as a poet through Whitman might seem odd. While he celebrated his own homoeroticism and independence from institutions, including that of marriage, Whitman had no sense of what it means to be crushed by them. He deals sensitively with death and loss, but there is little place for fear, anger, defeat and despair in his vision. For this reason, women poets are more likely to find a kindred spirit in Whitman's contemporary Emily Dickinson who, in contrast to his flamboyant 'I am large . . . I contain multitudes', murmured in short and laconic poems, 'I'm nobody', and yet spoke eloquently about the politics of power and what it means to be powerless as a woman, even at home.

Whitman may not be a poet for all feminists even though he considered *Leaves of Grass* 'essentially a woman's book', but Alicia Ostriker, the feminist poet and critic, believes that Whitman has been, both for her own poetry and for the poetry of many other American women, 'the exemplary precursor, killer of the censor and clearer of ground'. Both Ostriker and Kamala Das read Whitman when they were fourteen. And like Kamala Das, who felt that Whitman was closer to her than her own father because he 'spoke to me answering all the unasked questions lurking in my mind', Alicia Ostriker, too, felt that 'like some improbably open-minded parent', Whitman 'would permit everything. He permitted love . . . The degree and quantity and variety of love in Whitman are simply astonishing.' For a city girl, reading through Whitman in Manhattan's Central Park was 'to experience self-recognition', and to be 'given permission to exist by "Song of Myself."'[64] The Whitman that Kamala Das encountered, with

> that averted face, that casual look was enough to cause a disturbance that must last a lifetime. With him I exult in being alive physically, in being able to see the world as he saw it *possessing the good of the earth and sun*, exulting in my *identity received by my body*, exulting in the fact that *I do not crave for riches safe and palling nor the tame enjoyment* . . .

Maya Angelou, the African American poet, discovered Shakespeare—'my first white love'—as a child and credited him, along with Paul Laurence Dunbar, with forming her 'writing ambition' and for inspiring love for herself and confidence in her own strong spirit.

For the poet in Kamala Das, Whitman was her 'first white love', so to speak, pushing Byron's picture aside as a mere infatuation. As she recalled in 2007, like a 'tethered goat', she 'in [adolescent] hunger ate *Leaves of Grass*'. She had instinctively identified herself with his expansive vision and the free verse, direct and non-referential, which he created for the expression of his persona; his poems, as she puts it, 'loose-knit like the shuffling walk of a tramp', relying on internal discipline, discarding rhyme or metre, often using repetition, and a roll-call manner of enumerating or invoking place-names and objects to create a sense of motion and space. It is likely that some of her stylistic features—the omnivorous 'I', recurrent dialogue with the sea as a friend/confidant, her triple repetition of a word or phrase for emphasis—owe at least subconscious affinity to Whitman.

Kamala Das and the Love-ethic of Romantic Poetry

Whether it is the sun-drenched abundance of *Summer in Calcutta*, or the sombre seascape of *The Descendants*, or the old playhouse of the mind, or the lyrical resilience of the Anamalai sequence, or her return, from time to time, to the Radha–Krishna paradigm, or the poems occasioned by the 'gigantic deep-freeze' of 'the Canadian silence', the love-ethic—romantic, physical, spiritual, devotional and empathetic—is at the centre of her poetry.

In an interview in 1972, Kamala Das explained how the origins of *Summer in Calcutta* lay in a developing love relationship:

> In 1963 in Calcutta once again I came into contact with a man who had hurt me when I was fourteen years old. Some strange alchemy had changed fear into love. I was dismayed to find that I loved him, and I wanted to get him at any cost. I plunged head-long into an undignified ill-fated love-affair, moving about like a sleep-walker to meet him in the hot afternoons at strange places. Perhaps that rude summer crept into every line of poetry I wrote then.[65]

Earlier, in a letter of 10 December 1968, Kamala Das had stated the same source of inspiration but, apropos of my sharp criticism of some of the poems in *The Descendants*, she attributed the 'falling-off' in her poetry, paradoxically, to a 'curled like an old mongrel' contentment in love:

> I wrote the poems in *Summer in Calcutta* only to make a man love me, to break down his resistance. It was not my plan to become a poet, or even a personality. Last year two things have happened to me. I recovered from a prolonged illness, and returned from the hospital. The man became more or less mine. I am aware that I have become more integrated, more feminine. But I also know that my writing has disintegrated . . . I am full of this happy love, and the shabby smugness of it.

Looking back, in 2006, in a documentary film on her by Suresh Kohli, Kamala Das reiterated the paradox:

> If I had been a loved person I would not have become a writer. I would have been a happy human being. I would write about the calm. I would write about happiness, and a lovely love life and to want to live so that it would be an incentive for life.[66]

Whether her gloss is factually true or part invention or entirely fictional is less important here. What is more important is the connection she seemed to be positing between the writing of poetry and the discontentment or loss of love.

Is romantic poetry, and love poetry in particular, nourished by dissatisfaction, a sense of unattained or unattainable love and happiness? Is the poet like Keats's 'Bold Lover', who 'never, never canst kiss, / Though winning near the goal'? W.B. Yeats asserts that his poetic endeavour had been to win the love of one woman but considers the paradox that if he had won her he 'might have thrown poor words away / And been content to live'. The question 'Does the imagination dwell the most / Upon a woman won or woman lost?' haunted Yeats throughout his long poetic career, despite a happy marriage and fame. To take another example, Robert Graves, one of the finest English love poets, mythologized the source of his poetic inspiration as 'an invocation of the White Goddess, or Muse, the Mother of All Living . . . whose embrace is death'. He attributed his 'health' as a poet to his 'mistrust of the comfortable-point-of-rest', and to compulsive 'dwelling upon discomfort and terror'.

There are many factors that might explain why such a 'comfortable point of rest' is elusive in Kamala Das's poetry. Among the many causes of her unhappiness was certainly her near-death illness when she was in her thirties that extended her focus on the body from being a site of celebration to being a bearer of surgical and psychological scars. Both her illness and her survival inspired several poems such as 'Ischaemia in August', 'The Intensive Cardiac Care Unit', and, in fact, enlarged the sexual trope of 'my sad woman-body [that] felt beaten' to a sense of the body as a site of spiritual dialogue. 'Illness has become my mate, bound by ties of blood and nerves and bone, and, I hold with it long conversations.' 'The sensuous woman must choose her illness as she / Chooses her clothes to suit her own style.'

Illness also signifies loss of a kind: the existentialist fear of losing the body that you love. There is a sense of being reborn through reliving the body's beautiful past, or hoping and looking for its rebirth through dying. Kamala Das remarked in 2006: 'My poetry is an answer to the question [of happiness] that plagued me all my life.' When Kamala Das's American friend and publisher Andrew Arkin wrote that the poems of *Cinderella in Disguise* were 'all sad' and entreated her to 'write a poem at least once of happiness', she countered: 'Happiness? Where is that substance found? Is it available in the USA?'[67] One could not write a poem of happiness at will but one had to wait for it, if it came at all: 'I have been lucky, dying and resurrecting myself again and again.'

Kamala Das can take us to the brink of sadness and leave us, on the precipice as it were, wondering 'what is happiness?' In 'The Corridors' the speaker asks: 'Why do I so often in / Dreams linger at strange doorways, / Lonely to the bone, feeling / like an imposter . . . ?' 'The Bangles' opens with a startling question: 'Where does a woman go who is / Loved but finds love not enough'. Her woman persona in her various contexts is like 'a vessel overflowing with emotions' and thus predisposed to plenitude, and agonized by a constant sense of loss, even 'the loss of a love that I never once received'. Every now and then, her poems take on the tone of stocktaking, dwelling on love lost than love won, balancing loss against the gain, and an increasing belief in a continuing search. 'Gracious Allah', a later poem, ruminates on 'A life / that had had almost all / but love . . .'

The poet mythicized her 'looking' for the unrequited, absent, lost or unattainable love. She described this search as a 'wayward search for love', but also added, 'all searches are wayward'. 'Love was the only religion I ever recognised,' as she reiterates in 'March of the Mercenaries', a poem written after her conversion to Islam but the answers offered by organized religion did not satisfy her, just as they did not in 'The Inheritance', a 1967 poem. In two of her last poems 'A Timepiece' and 'Ya Allah', she claims that 'I cannot fold / My wayward limbs to crawl into / Coffins of religions' and that she never learnt from Islam, either, 'a clean way to compromise'. Equally, although she kept a Krishna image in her room, her use of the Radha–Krishna motif is mythical rather than religious in the conventional sense. In 'Radha', the mystic union is reached through a distinctly eroticized diction and rhythm: a run-on sequence of alternating short and long lines builds the space of waiting and frantic expectation which in the last four lines slowly dissolves, holding back briefly at 'but', before folding headlong into the singular 'You', the last monosyllabic line:

The long waiting
Had made their bond so chaste, and all the doubting
And the reasoning
So that in his first true embrace, she was girl
And virgin crying
Everything in me
Is melting, even the hardness at the core
O Krishna, I am melting, melting, melting
Nothing remains but
You.

The poetic vocation is, as Seamus Heaney puts it, 'a journey where each point of arrival—whether in one's poetry or one's life—turned out to be a stepping stone rather than a destination'. Kamala Das's Anamalai sequence is a moving exploration of this kind and records a twofold journey, an outward and uphill, and an inward and downhill. The woman 'wrapped in the shroud of betrayals' climbing the hills, with an accompanying mist that has 'no kinship with the hills' but has a 'blood-tie' with her, to hear the silence of the 'deaf-mute' mountain, and as its fog ascends the stairways of the sky, let 'the flesh of her spirit [be] but its flesh'. The inward journey is 'the most tortuous', 'the longest route home and the steepest descent'. In the last section, the speaker recognizes the 'greater love' when 'some unknown womb shall begin to *convulse* / to welcome your restructured perfection' (italics mine). However, the preceding section ruefully admits that it is in early youth or in 'weary old age' that one experiences life's true meaning whereas 'The middle is an opaque / glass pane, muddied by fingerprints'. Kamala Das was fifty-one when she wrote the sequence. While 'the greater love' still 'awaits you where the red road finally ends',

> In meaninglessness, trapped, I must
> so remain and taste the outer
> rind of human pain and the seeds
> of mirthless laughter.

The movement is circular rather than linear; the eleven poems fluctuate between the outer and inner journeys, of ascent and descent, of real loss and hopeful gain. Being a votary of love, as Kamala Das insisted, 'When I loved, / I became pure love, / when I lost / I became pure loss, / nothing else.' But what is the complex stretch between these two poles? In this sense, in the 'ruffled sea' of her poetic journey, the Anamalai sequence forms an island of cherished retreat and contemplative lyricism.

The Unfinished Woman

The Unfinished Women is the suggestive title of an exhibition of her paintings of nude women held in Cochin in 1994. These paintings are emblematic of the incompleteness implicit in Kamala Das's love-ethic. In an interview, she explained that while 'nudity is a costume for innocence' they were all sad and incomplete women because the same beautiful body was also the cause of their suffering.[68] Clearly, she was alluding to the emotional and psychological ruptures linked to a woman's physical suffering. Kamala Das once remarked: 'I have always regarded the hospital as a planet situated like a sandwich filling between the familiar earth and the strange domain of death . . . I have often wished to take myself apart and stick all the bits, the heart, the intestines, the liver, the reproductive organs, the skin, the hair and all the rest on a large canvas to form a collage which could then be donated to my readers.' This is similar to what the Mexican artist Frida Kahlo does in her paintings such as *Henry Ford Hospital* and *The Two Fridas*. The former shows a naked Kahlo on a hospital bed with several items such as a fetus, a flower, a pelvis floating around her and connected to her by red vein-like strings. *The Two Fridas* portrays the 'unloved' Frida, with a damaged heart, in a white dress stained with spots of blood, side by side with the 'loved' Frida, with a normal heart, dressed in bright colours. However, Kamala did not fulfil her intention of painting a woman's dismembered body but some of her 'Illness' poems such as 'I Shall Not Forget' and 'Death Is So Mediocre' portray the scarred and damaged body in their surrealist collocation of images of illness, rotting limbs, 'the slow unwrapping of the carcass'.

Kahlo's themes, too, were love, loss, surgery, politics and an ambivalent attachment to an older husband. Kamala Das admired the unprecedented 'savage candour' of Kahlo's self-portraits. Reading her biography, she 'experienced another incarnation', 'wearied' by Kahlo's sufferings and 'yet strangely stimulated by her genius', and by her bold paintings especially of her own birth, the foetus thrusting itself out of her mother's body.

She did suggest that there were two Kamalas, the loved and unloved versions. These versions incorporated varied identities—Amy, Madhavikutty and Suraiya—which she explored and tried to reconcile through writing, although the unloved version or its persona seems to be more predominant than the other. Describing herself as 'a very incomplete person . . . [but] growing, changing, altering', Kamala Das also claimed a life of unfinishedness both for her poems and her paintings: 'I believe in leaving a poem

A relationship

This love older than I by myriad
Saddened centuries was once a prayer
In his bones that made them grow in years of
Adolescence to this favoured height. Yes,
It was my desire that made him male
And beautiful, so that when at last we met
To believe that once I knew not his
Form, his quiet touch, or the blind kindness
Of his lips was hard indeed. Betray me?
Yes, he can, but never physically
Only with words that curl their limbs at
Touch of air and die with metallic sighs.
Why care I for their quick sterile sting while
My body's wisdom tells and tells again
That I shall find my rest, my sleep, my peace
And even death nowhere else but here in
My betrayer's arms . . .

41

'"A Relationship": Text and Drawing', Kamala Das. 23 July 1978. Courtesy: Devindra Kohli.

incomplete . . . It is completed in the reader's mind. Deliberately I've left my poems, stories and painting incomplete.'[69] Although a characteristic feature of her poems has always been to 'voice' questions, as though in a dialogue with herself, and leave a mist of uncertainty, she articulated this interface between the unfinished woman and the unfinished poem first in 1990: 'A woman writer unfrustrates herself by writing of a life she desires . . . She seeks to complete her life and to perfect herself through her writings.'[70] That this notion was a concern of hers even much earlier is suggested by her drawing, in 1978, of the figure of the lower part of a woman over the text of 'A Relationship' in this editor's copy of *The Old Playhouse and Other Poems*. The half figure of the woman seems to emerge from the text/body of the poem.[71] The poem celebrates the archetypal love of man and woman and the female desire that shapes it and makes the man 'male and beautiful'. Does the poem complete the woman's body or does her incomplete body complete the poem?

When Yeats speaks of the conflicting choice between 'perfection of the life, or of the work' which the intellect of man is forced to make, he is presumably speaking from a male poet's point of view because a woman poet, especially the housewife, would have other roles to perfect herself in before she can choose the perfection of the work, as Ruth Whitman persuasively argues from her own experience in 'The Divided Heart'.[72] Am I going to be me, or am I going to be a mother? Am I going to be me, or a wife? Such questions would not agonize a Yeats as they would a Sylvia Plath. Kamala Das often said that she would have been content just being a loved daughter, a loved mother and a loved wife. She may have been all these, especially when seen through the eyes of her parents, her husband and her sons. But if she had been all that, would she still have been content and thrown poor words away?

In 'Sleeping in the Moonlight', first published in 1996, Kamala Das recollects that when she was fourteen, they were told that to sleep in moonlight would be to invite madness. Unlike her brother, who she claims was 'wise and careful', she did the opposite and slept one night in the open quadrangle of Nalapat in order to feel how 'the ripened moon, trapped / In the horned branches of the jack tree / blanched the sky and cooled my skin'. That incident reconfirms how strong her desire was to experience 'I am different / I am an entity'. To unwrap 'the whatness of me within' from 'all the layers of sham grown like skins', therefore, was a way of 'unfrustrating' herself through her poetry by writing of the desired life, and thereby completing herself.

As we can see, contradictions abound in Kamala Das. She confronts and critiques the male figures, the father, the husband and the lover for her 'unloved' self but also desires to fulfil herself through their love. She invokes Krishna, her mythical lover, with his infidelities, who is beloved by Radha, an older married woman. And yet, in her novella *A Doll for the Child Prostitute* (1977), originally published as a short story—'Cages'—and made into a National Award–winning film by K.P. Kumaran, the prostitute is named Meera, with subversive irony, who out of love secretly marries a young student-client only to return to her trade soon after because he abandons her: 'Is it not strange that I am Meera and he is Krishna?' But a stranger paradox posed here is the failure to 'wed' the real love to the mythical in a humdrum life which lacks it. Another child prostitute who is sold by her mother to a brothel-keeper is named Rukmini, which is also the name of the principal wife of Krishna.

Commenting on her painting entitled *The Widow*, she remarked: 'Everything is hidden, the eyes alone are revealed. I've always loved the *purdah*, a kind of *prachanna vesham* (fancy dress, mask), I am going to draw women in purdah singing, dancing. It will be dramatic.'[73] During her stay in Colombo at the time of the civil war, whenever she went out, as a survival strategy she wore a burqa. Fifteen years later, after her conversion to Islam, she controversially defended the burqa by saying: 'Modernity is in the thinking . . . I would have worn granite to please the man I loved. In surrendering to love I am not incomplete like my poems. I surrender completely.'[74]

With her suspicion of dogmatic binaries, as noted earlier, she never felt comfortable with being described as a feminist. Although she critiques patriarchy for its insensitive and loveless structures, in her empathetic, egalitarian vision gender is inconsequential and only love and mutual respect are the binding forces. If in Kerala she felt inhibited 'like an Egyptian mummy all wrapped up in lint', in her English poetry the same 'outcast' could yet wrap the contradictions of her life around herself 'like a shawl' and keep herself warm, as Alice Walker urges in her celebrated poem 'Be Nobody's Darling'.[75]

Knitting/Unknitting the Knot of Contrarieties

I have attempted to signpost some biographical and literary factors that have had a bearing on the making of Kamala Das as a poet. I have drawn on her published and unpublished writings, her letters to me and, occasionally, to others, and on our conversations of thirty years. The questions of selfhood, identity, language and ambivalence in relationships, involving familial, sexual, spiritual and egalitarian love, which she raises and explores are engaging enough. However, her sudden shifts in manner and voice, tone and syntax, imagery and rhythm, so characteristic of her, surprise with freshness but they also disconcert anyone expecting compliance with formalist poetics.

These shifts and turns certainly surprised me when as a young lecturer in English, brought up on the then influential New Criticism (still valuable in my view), and imbued with admiration that I still have for such diverse poets as Shakespeare, Donne, Coleridge, Keats, Hardy, Hopkins, Yeats, Eliot, Whitman, Dickinson and Frost, I stumbled on the refreshing, homespun and unpretentious but audacious poems in *Summer in Calcutta*. That was 1966. In a similar vein, the poet Meena Alexander recounts how in 1973, with a British PhD on Romantic literature, Kamala Das's poems 'spoke to her' when she first read *The Old Playhouse and Other Poems*: 'There was something passionate in the lilt of that voice . . . made me stop still in my tracks.' Among the younger generation, two outstandingly promising poets who acknowledge their debt to Kamala are Meena Kandasamy who is grateful for 'the courage I find in [Kamala's] powerful verse', and Tishani Doshi who discovered her poetic self through Kamala's poems: 'alive' and 'both an invocation and an invitation'.

Indeed, Kamala Das speaks to us; that is the spirit in which her poems were conceived and written and that is how they work, engaging, conversational, at times sounding like one of our own dreams. Her omnipresent 'I' confides, intrudes, shocks. It is a sentimental, flamboyant, histrionic, confessional, melodramatic, rebellious and devotional but quintessentially an empathetic 'I'. It befriends us but rarely comforts us because it is not meant to, asking questions in a dialogue of one, or in a dialogue with the reader, or the tree, or the city, or the sea, or the forest, but always in her inimitable voice, not adopted from literary, historical and philosophical traditions to achieve a referential effect.

Writing in 1969, David McCutchion reminded both Indian and non-Indian readers and critics that 'English poetic rhythms are notoriously difficult' for Indian poets or for that matter Scottish and Welsh poets to imitate, as the rhythms and intonation of their own languages are quite different from those of English.[76] He went on to commend the naturally 'cautious' decision by Kamala Das in 'choosing a conversational free verse line' thereby achieving 'the freedom and originality of being unreservedly' herself. This decision to follow her own speech rhythms in her verse is what Raja Rao pioneered in his first novel, *Kanthapura* (1938). Basing it on the premise that Indians 'are all instinctively bilingual', he proposed:

> The tempo of Indian life must be infused into our English expression, even as the tempo of American or Irish life has gone into the making of theirs. We, in India, think quickly, we talk quickly, and when we move we move quickly. There must be something in the sun of India that makes us rush and tumble and run on . . . We have neither punctuation nor the treacherous 'ats' and 'ons' to bother us—we tell the interminable tale.

Run-on line is a distinctive feature of Kamala Das's poems, and to the 'treacherous' prepositions we may add the definite article which she often skips and felt that her line was more effective that way. Clearly flouting formalist poetics, Kamala Das dared to attempt the apparently arbitrary and instinctively authentic, which explains the mixed critical response to her poetry. While Carol Rumens appreciates the 'darker, subtler nuances' of her imagery, the Virginia Woolf–like poetic stream of consciousness of her descriptive mode, as well as the 'obliqueness' of her vital poetic voice, she finds Kamala Das's 'vernacular oddities', enjambing, and her style of not breaking the poem into stanzas distracting.[77] Chris Wallace-Crabbe, however, defends her metonymic style, her signature enjambement, her 'lacunae, her little rows of dots' and 'syntactical swerves' as 'acts of resistance', rather than weaknesses, worked to advantage.[78] Keki Daruwalla praises the achieved excellence of some of her poems such as 'Evening at the Old Malabar House', 'The House Builders', and 'Ferns', as well as Das's sensitivity to the victimized but he finds her use of mixed metaphor less satisfying and her poetry lacking in sustained achievement and equipoise. Krishna Rayan, on the other hand, defends the mixed metaphor in Kamala Das as a peculiarity of a modernist sensibility, invoking examples from Dylan Thomas and Shakespeare. A mixed metaphor is by definition and design a yoking together of incompatible images or metaphors.

Precisely because of her apparent arbitrariness in form and style much criticism on her, even when favourable, has concentrated on the autobiographical and 'confessional' aspects of her work. M. Sivaramakrishna has even argued that 'Those who look for . . . imagistic novelty, structural variation and thematic range in Mrs. Das' poetry are looking for elements which are non-essential from her perspective. In effect, the quality of experience becomes the sole criterion and this experience in Mrs. Das is concerned invariably with love.'[79]

It is hoped that this selection of Kamala Das's poems offers enough variety for a reader to discover how in unexpected ways her poetry shows stylistic features such as alliteration, assonance, internal and end rhyme, imagistic novelty and structural variation. In several poems, Kamala Das used the traditional stanza form to develop and modulate her theme, as in 'Someone Else's Song', 'With Its Quiet Tongue', 'The Corridors', 'My Morning Tree' and 'Afterwards'. Even in poems which are not broken into stanzas, as indeed most of her poems are not, she can by change in rhythm and occasional use of rhymes in response to the speaking voice create a stylistic variation within the same poem. See 'The Bison at the Water's Edge', which opens with a faint echo of Sylvia Plath:

> Who says a marriage must mean only two?
> The clement climate of mine was due
> Not to one man alone, but two,
> Two dissimilar co-tenants
> In one cramped room.

Analogous to Emily Dickinson's frequent use of the dash as her 'stylistic signature', Kamala Das uses unconventional punctuation, three dots either in the middle of a line, before the start of the next sentence, or at the end of the poem, suggesting a pause, continuity or incompleteness. She employs long lines alternating with short lines, colloquial language and an interactive tone. Her enjambement propels the reader forward through the poem and keeps us reading. To illustrate her thematic range and stylistic variation, one might look closely at three poems: 'The Dance of the Eunuchs', 'An Introduction' and the little-known 'Woman without Her Shadow'.

In 'The Dance of the Eunuchs' there are three shifts in the portrayal of the dance as the poet moves from the dance to the dancers. The opening long sentence flowing through eight frantic run-on lines conveys the swirling movement ('wide skirts going round and round') and the accompanying dissonance through phrasal repetition and assonance ('cym*bals* / Rich*ly* *clash*ing, and an*klets* jingling, jingling / Jingling'). After a pause signalled by a row of three dots, the flamboyant event is briskly linked to the flaming gulmohur, before the whirling momentum resumes in lines 5–6: 'long braids flying, dark eyes flashing', echoing 'richly clashing' cymbals. There is a momentary softer touch, through internal rhyming, in 'jasmines in their *hair*, some / *Were* dark and some *were* almost *fair*' before tone and rhythm change again, just when the focus shifts, empathetically, to their melancholy songs and their inner 'drought'. Although the dance and music are, as expected, brusque yet there is no clapping, no excitement around. The dance contracts to mere 'convulsions' and the audience to 'so silent' crows and so 'wide eyed, still' children. For the observing, empathizing poet, the real or symbolic relief turns out to be 'a meagre rain' smelling of the urine of lizards and mice, which like 'mere drizzle' in her short story 'The Sandal Trees' signifies inadequacy and unfulfilled desires.[80]

'An Introduction', the only Asian poem included in *The Norton Anthology of Literature by Women* (edited by Sandra Gilbert and Susan Gubar 1985, 1996), is arguably Kamala Das's minor 'Song of Myself', although she might as well have called it 'Poem of Myself', or just 'Myself, an Indian Poet', using the reflexive pronoun the way many Indians sometimes use it. The opening lines which introduce the regional, multilingual background of an Indian poet from Malabar are disarming in tone and modest in content. The mode changes as the poet engages with the carping 'they' over *any* writer's freedom to choose his/her language. It is a spirited defence, argumentative in tone, carried through analogy and phrasal repetition. But in the heat of polemics, she slips in internal rhyming ('the speech of the mind that is / *Here* and not *there*, a mind that sees and hears and / Is *aware*') to emphasize that the poet's language is not just a blind and deaf outpouring of emotion. The speaker-poet, seemingly innocent of politics at the beginning, has been drawn into making a political statement.

The abrupt 'I was child' in the middle of line 23 signals an emotional rupture, as the voice shifts from a fluent linguistic defence to the autobiographical past. The area of conflict with the disapproving 'they' widens to include 'he' from the familial/

social/hetero-patriarchal order. Her innocent childhood ended suddenly when 'they told me' of her pubertal maturation and married her off prematurely. The line break here creates ambiguity. This allows, as Rosemary Marangoly George has also noted, 'a syntactically awkward heterosexual reading' implying that the 'youth of sixteen' whom 'he' draws into the bedroom is necessarily 'I', the child bride, or a grammatically correct reading and thereby making 'a fluent statement about same-sex desire that competes with the young bride's heterosexual ineptness'.[81] Instead of the love that she wanted she experienced rejection, not physical but psychological.

After the resultant blenching at her womanliness, as the self tries to recover and rebuild, it faces greater fragmentation through multiple gendered roles which 'they' assign to her one name, the wife. One way to rebuild the self and transcend the role playing is through poetry and the creative use of language that goes beyond individual identity by making the specific general through shared human nature and experience. Correspondingly, there is another shift in mood and tone, indicated by her characteristic row of three dots before 'I met a man, loved him'. Recognizing its innate capacity to rebuild, the poetic 'I' reasserts to be embodied in others and others being embodied in her: all contradictory parts woven into the same chain. 'I project myself—also I return—I am with you, and know how it is.' That is how Whitman's poetic 'I' 'knitted the old knot of contrariety' in 'Crossing Brooklyn Ferry', a poem which Kamala Das acknowledged she had read.

'Woman without Her Shadow' (reprinted here for the first time since it was published in 1984) is analogous to Emily Dickinson's 'Because I could not stop for Death' which narrates a woman's romantic ride on a carriage with a kindly suitor who personifies death. Kamala Das dramatizes an old and ailing woman's experience of death, using her shadow as a conceit.

Unable to travel herself, the woman sends her shadow instead to be with her lonely lover in another city. When the shadow returns, also grown older, the woman feels vicariously gratified through its account of how well it looked after her lover's needs. This narrative motif makes the reader, too, an interested listener. The woman and her shadow converge again just as she, like a mermaid, runs down 'the fearsome stairways of the sea', and joyously experiences death, with a sense of release and envisioned blooming of witch azaleas. Framed in a reverie, as the dying woman hears one last time her lover moan in his siesta, the reader, through this ingenious twist to the conceit, remains involved in the narrative of death as a sensuous and romantic love experience.

Reclaiming/Subverting the Muse?

Kamala Das, naturally, wrote as a woman and about being a woman but her exploration of the nature of love, of death and of the need of empathy speaks to any reader irrespective of gender. It was not to the poetry of Sarojini Naidu and Toru Dutt in English or that of her mother in Malayalam that Kamala turned to for stimulus; in fact, she rebelled against them to chart her own territory, and she found Meera's devotional poetry lacking in physicality. 'My Grandmother's House' and 'Blood' are outstanding tributes to her bloodlines, to the lost matriarchal traditions, as well as to her grandmother to whom she related emotionally rather than intellectually. There are two poems 'My Mother at Sixty-Six' and 'Alzheimer's' in which her mother presides 'pale as a late winter's moon', and 'The Time of the Drought' and 'Grandmothers' in which she has a mild presence, although Balamani Amma wrote a moving poem (when Kamala Das was seriously ill in 1965) lauding Kamala Das's poetic power to transform 'the worms gnawing at her core . . . into butterflies'. On the other hand, there are four longish poems about her rocky relationship with her father, besides at least three in which the father's presence is felt, including 'Glass' with its concluding line, 'I've misplaced a father / Somewhere, and I look / For him everywhere'.

Clearly, her poetry, like that of many 'confessional' poets, male and female, lends itself to or invites a Freudian interpretation but like any other pigeonholing approach it is useful only up to a point. One consequence of Kamala Das's male-centred love-ethic is the opposing positions of men and women critics, as for example in the readings of two poets and academics, Vincent O'Sullivan and Shirley Geok-lin Lim.

Vincent O'Sullivan explores ways to unify the apparent contradictions in her poetry and her autobiography. Being rooted in the Indian cultural tradition, Kamala Das avoids binary opposites which have characterized much of Western feminism, and the paradigm of the myth of Krishna provides artistic cogency to her bold portrayal of infidelity and of her pursuit of love. O'Sullivan believes that 'Das must be read as a religious poet, if she is to be read correctly.'

Shirley Geok-lin Lim, however, argues against reading Das's best work as an allegorical portrayal of Radha worshiping Krishna because the mythical paradigm represents 'the authoritative word' of patriarchy against which Kamala Das's persona rebels. Rejecting Freudian and Lacanian approaches, Lim sees instead in Kamala Das a Bakhtinian model of 'the internal dialogism of double-voiced' narrative. At the centre of the poetics of Kamala Das's work, according to her, is the female self as 'desiring' subject seeking 'satisfaction', using 'satisfaction' epistemologically, to include the idea of sexual desire as well as fulfilment of the protagonist's inner 'identity needs'. When Kamala Das's narrator speaks of her admiring readers as lovers, the desire to write may be interpreted as 'the desire for a collective libidinous intercourse, a female exposure fantasy' which ironically falls within the terms of 'patriarchal inter(discourse)'. In a sociopolitical repressive world 'satisfaction' for the woman as empowered writer remains elusive.

K. Satchidanandan notes the widening of Kamala Das's concerns through extension of her sympathies to suffering humanity, and argues that because she is the inheritor of many Indian traditions, including the multilayered tradition of Indian women's poetry, Kamala Das celebrates 'the greatness of love that even while being expressed through the body also transcends the body'.

The poet Hoshang Merchant, once a member of Kamala Das's Bahutantrika, wrote a poignant sequence of poems in memoriam. In his prose obituary he found it logical that Kamala Das identified Krishna in her new young Moslem lover/husband. 'She had reached "the other shore" in her devotion to him/Him. Barely a few years before she had become the old Radha who had to hide her face from strangers who would mock her for becoming an old crone from being Krishna's beloved in her youth ("The Cobwebs"). But now resplendent in Layla's veil she calls to Love Himself from the other shore.'

What happens to the woman, the woman poet, the female soul, who is again betrayed and abandoned by this new he/He that Merchant is referring to? Kamala's last poems, such as 'March of the Mercenaries', 'A Timepiece', 'The Munafique' and 'The Magnolia', written between 2005 and 2007 and published posthumously, confront this betrayal and its agonizing ambivalence, reconfirming that the poet's search and journey continued till the very end. In an interview in 2000, the period Hoshang Merchant has in mind, Kamala Das asserted:

> Krishna was my playmate. My grandmother had told me that he would marry me. I still talk to him all the time. He's aware of all that's happening in my life. When in difficulty it's still him I call out to, not Allah.[82]

Among the last poems mentioned above is also 'Radha's Dream' in which Kamala Das returns explicitly to the Radha–Krishna paradigm, as she seems to have done in nine such poems written at different and ostensibly key stages in her life: 'Radha Krishna' (*Summer in Calcutta*), 'Radha' and 'The Maggots' (*The Descendants*), 'A Phantom-Lotus', 'Ghanashyam' and 'Radha' (*Tonight, This Savage Rite*), 'Krishna' (*Collected Poems* vol. I), 'Vrindavan' (*The Best of Kamala Das*), 'The Cobwebs' (*Only the Soul Knows How to Sing*) and 'Radha's Dream' (*Closure*).

The quest for the male lover/god led Meera, Akkamahadevi and Andal to relinquish their homes and husbands and live the life of ascetics and wandering devotees. For Kamala, in contrast, living a life of enforced austerity, dressing only in white, which she called the colour of mourning, or in monochromatic clothes, relinquishing jewellery was uncongenial. Yet, as with these women saint-poets, 'it is the looking that makes the poet go on writing, searching. If you find *someone*, the search is over, poetry is over' (italics mine).

Poetry, like any other art form, cannot get written without inspiration. But what is the mysterious source of inspiration and where do its springs lie? Arguably, it is the unconscious apprehended by the conscious self. The unconscious has been perceived by Jung and many poets as symbolized by the sea, 'the mother of all that lives' or personified as the Muse. Given that our inherited world view and the history of our civilization have been shaped and written from the male point of view, male poets have used the image of the Muse as a loved object who inspires the male artist, whilst she herself remains silent and passive. 'Man Does, Woman Is' is the title poem of a collection by Robert Graves who mythologized this paradigm as the White Goddess, an idealized, powerful female figure whom he identified with the Muse, the inspirational source of his poetry. He said, 'The Muse is a deity, but she is also a woman.' This relationship is erotic and 'the White Goddess is anti-domestic; she is the perpetual other woman.'[83]

Many Western feminist poets such as Adrienne Rich and May Sarton have responded to this paradigm of the male poet and female Muse and have raised important questions about the gendering of creative inspiration. Agreeing with Graves's premise about the centrality of the erotic relationship between poet and Muse to the creative process, May Sarton's poems and her semi-autobiographical novel *Mrs. Stevens Hears the Mermaids Singing* (1975) offer a female response. Adrienne Rich and others, using revisionist readings, reclaim the Muse as an active figure through metaphors of motherhood, sisterhood and female lovers or invoke female literary or mythological figures such as Sappho who was named the Tenth Muse by Plato. Paradoxically, Sappho herself invoked the Muses: 'Girls, chase the violet-bosomed Muses' bright / Gifts and the plangent lyre, lover of hymns', and the high quality of her poetry was acknowledged even by Graves who maintained that a woman poet should write as a woman and 'not as if she was an honorary man'.[84] Whitman believed, unconditionally, that as poets and artists 'women create, as man creates'. Or is feminine sexuality / sensibility, intrinsically, a 'capacious and embracing hermaphrodite awareness', as Rukmini Bhaya Nair, invoking Sappho, proffers?[85]

Did Kamala Das have a Muse? The American scholar and critic Bruce King sees Kamala Das's most remarkable achievement as writing in an Indian English, with a distinct vocabulary, idioms, choice of verbs, syntactical constructions, directness of expression, and natural, idiomatic and colloquial vigour. As a female poet, he argues, she could achieve this liberation from a conscious, formalized British speech and diction in the mid-1960s more naturally than her male counterparts could, because it was also part of her rebellion against the traditional role of Indian women and their 'fight against the kind of diction [which] was associated with a conformity of behaviour and attitudes'.[86] Commenting on her uneven poetic achievement, he describes her as 'always a hit-or-miss poet, who wrote regularly but trusted the muse more than revision'.

Although King uses the term 'muse' with a touch of gentle irony, the questions which he as well as feminist poets, critics and revisionists raise are relevant to Kamala's poetry and her views on the source of her inspiration. Is the Muse who inspires female poets different from the Muse who inspires male poets? Is the Muse who inspires a woman poet necessarily female, passive or active? Or may a female poet, such as Kamala Das, who is a victim of patriarchy and its staunch critic, still 'look for' and find creative inspiration in her love for a man/male god?

Who was Kamala Das's Muse? In the French novel which had unforgettably devastated her as an adolescent in Malabar, the young des Grieux sees in Manon Lescaut 'that divine form, that inexhaustible store of enchantments of the perfidious lover to which we feel drawn'. If Graves's Goddess is anti-domestic, is Krishna the perpetual other man/male god in Kamala Das's love-ethic? 'Vrindavan lives on in every woman's mind / And the flute luring her / From home and her husband . . .'

The relationship of a poet, male or female, to the domestic is worth considering. In a conversation with me, Kamala Das postulated conflicting claims on being a poet and on being a daughter, wife and mother. She reiterated this to Merrily Weisbord:

> A writer moves away from family, old relationships, very far with the speed of a falling star. Otherwise the writer is destroyed, and only the member of the family remains: the mother, sister, daughter, wife. The writer at some point must ask: Do I want to be a well-loved member of the family? Or do I want to be a good writer? You can't be both at the same time.[87]

In *My Story* too, grappling with a sense of fragmentation and death, Kamala Das had reflected on the unreality of familial relationships and, in a leave-taking gesture, checking her spiritual equipment of 'condemning none, understanding all', was preparing for the final 'fondling' by Him:

> In actuality who is he [husband]? Who am I? Who are these three boys who call themselves my children? We are burdened with perishable bodies which strike up bonds which are also unreal, and perishable. The only relationship that is permanent is the one which we form with God. My mate is He. He shall come to me in myriad shapes. In many shapes shall I surrender to His desire. I shall be fondled by Him. I shall be betrayed by Him. I shall pass through all the pathways of this world, *condemning none, understanding all* and then become part of Him. Then for me there shall be no return journey . . . (italics mine)

In seeking to find the ideal in the real, Krishna in the husband/lover, the Muse in the domestic, was Kamala Das looking for an incompatible combination? The conflicting claims, however, did not prevent her from fulfilling her roles in both the domestic and artistic spheres.

Her youngest son, Jaisurya Das, cherishes Kamala Das as mother and is aware that 'she was more of a poet . . . [who] always treated poetry and prose differently . . . poetry she lived, prose was her creative instinct.'[88] Her eldest son, M.D. Nalapat, however, claims that he knew Kamala Das only as mother and not as writer: 'Amma is no poet, no writer, no campaigner for women's rights. She is Amma.' And when asked to single out one outstanding quality of Kamala Das, he hit the nail on the head:

> What I remember about her is that she had no prejudices. She was willing to believe that every individual, every human being had good and bad qualities and that the good qualities were better than the bad qualities. So in that sense, even the people who hurt her she found it difficult to dislike them or hate them. And when they made the slightest show of reconciliation to her she completely forgave all the past and after that she became quite friendly with them. So that was her biggest quality, the quality of forgiveness, and the quality of understanding that human beings can make mistakes, that human beings are capable sometimes of emotion that is not worthy of them and that human beings can change and become a better person.[89]

That the rejection of hate is a conscious choice is evident in Kamala Das's poetry. She wrote: 'Hate is a thorn in the flesh. I don't want hate residing within me for anyone. That would ruin my attitude towards life.' That is the choice she foregrounded in a 1973 poem, refusing to walk 'with hearts grown scabrous with a hate', inherited as 'our father's lunacy speaking, / In different tones'—the muezzin's high wail, the Angelus, and the Brahmin's assonant chant—'babbling' the same message, 'slay the unbeliever'.

Dissenting from received religious traditions, especially sanctioned by patriarchy, and offering an unorthodox perspective is full of peril, as Emily Dickinson, too, was aware. 'The shore is safer', she wrote in 1850, 'but I love to buffet the sea—I can count the bitter wrecks here in these pleasant waters, and hear the murmuring winds, but oh, I love the danger.'

Instinctively, for Kamala Das the sea, as mentioned earlier, was a double metaphor. It was her compulsive expedition to 'fish out poetry'—from 'the ruffled sea' of her past—'That is neither glad / Nor sad / But can cut / Precisely the gut / To wake you / Out of dreams'. But the sea was also accommodating, transcending artificial divisions and reconciling binary opposites. Writing of poetry was also a reconciler and unifier: 'What I value more than anything while engaging in writing are emotional and spiritual benefits.' She even imagined, in one of her last poems, 'The last breath / Exhaled / Is the last poem / Released. Then / The curtain falls . . .'[90]

In his sensuous and reflective memorial tribute, 'The Reckoning', a fascinating twenty-line variation on the caudate sonnet, Jeet Thayil[91] captures both the subversive and reconciling aspects of Kamala Das's poetry and her life, as he envisions her reading about the Day of Reckoning and envisioning herself—self-aware and yielding—lifting *both hands* to receive the book of judgement, without a tremor, watching for the tremor. But in the *cauda* of the sonnet, in the world of the phones ringing and editors asking permissions, there is a tremor of a different kind, 'a noise like the sea / Crashing against the apartment's high windows'. And the poet answering how she missed love's yielding which like yielding to death, 'as child to mother's arms', she sang of in 'The Descendants': 'We were the yielders, / Yielding ourselves to everything.'

And in one of her last poems, breaking free from the noose of religion, Kamala Das had envisioned herself

To stand face to face
With God
Who knowing the answers
Asked no questions.
Love nourishes love.
It gnaws at the vitals
Of reason
And silences
Wth a kiss.[92]

Paderborn, August 2014

Notes

1. Eunice de Souza, ed., *Nine Indian Women Poets: An Anthology* (New Delhi: Oxford University Press, 1997), 8.

2. Margaret O'Donnell, ed., *An Anthology of Commonwealth Verse* (London: Blackie, 1963), xxi.

3. Devindra Kohli and Suresh Kohli, eds, 'Adil Jussawalla: Interview with Bruce King', *Indian Literary Review* IV, no. 1 (January 1986): 3–9.

4. Arvind Krishna Mehrotra, 'Introduction: Death of a Poet', in *Arun Kolatkar: Collected Poems in English*, ed. Arvind Krishna Mehrotra (Tarset, Northumberland: Bloodaxe Books, 2010), 25–26.

5. Devindra Kohli, 'Virgin Whiteness: An Interpretation of the Poetry of Kamala Das', *Literary Criterion* 7, no. 4 (1967): 64–79.

6. 'I write in rhyme and metre, which is passé these days. I go by what my heart tells me.' Vikram Seth quoted in Michael White, 'A Suitable Ploy', *Daily Telegraph*, 4 June 2006, http://www.telegraph.co.uk/culture/3652931/A-suitable-ploy.html (accessed on 9 August 2014).

7. R.W. Desai, 'But Where Is the Sculpture of Rhyme?', *Indian Literary Review* vol. I, no. 12 to vol. II, no. 1 (1979): 77–80.

8. Frank Kinahan, 'Artists on Art: An Interview with Seamus Heaney', *Critical Inquiry* 8, no. 3 (Spring 1982): 416.

9. Jeet Thayil, ed., *The Bloodaxe Book of Contemporary Indian Poets* (Tarset, Northumberland: Bloodaxe Books, 2008), 17.

10. 'Indian Poetry in English: Two Views', *Journal of Commonwealth Literature* 9, no. 1 (March 1974): 20–34.

11. *The Concise Encyclopedia of English and American Poets and Poetry*, 2nd ed., eds Stephen Spender and Donald Hall (London: Hutchinson, 1963, 1970).

12. Quoted in Sheela Reddy, 'Midnight's Orphans', *Outlook*, February 25 2002, http://www.outlookindia.com/article/Midnights-Orphans/214680 (accessed on 9 August 2014).

13. Ibid.

14. Erica Jong, 'The Artist as Housewife: The Housewife as Artist', in *Ms.* (October 1972), reprinted in *The First Ms. Reader*, ed. Francine Klagsbrun (New York: Warner, 1973), 111–22.

15. 'The Nalapat family needed at that time not any caste-snobbery but cash and commonsense.' Kamala Das, 'My Grandmother', *Imprint* (March 1974): 37–39. Cf. Kamala Das, *My Story* (New Delhi: Sterling, 1977, 1998), 4.

16. 'My Husband and the Co-operative Movement in India' (unpublished typescript in the editor's collection).

17. Kamala Das, 'My Grandmother', *Imprint* (March 1974): 37–39.

18. The child-wife of Madhav, as she explains in *Kamala Das: An Introduction* (a Sahitya Akademi documentary film), dir. Suresh Kohli.

19. See Kamala Das, 'The Fourteen Days' War', 'A Week with Manasi' and 'The Dispensary', in *Wages of Love: Uncollected Writings of Kamala Das*, ed. Suresh Kohli (Noida: HarperCollins, 2013).

20. Kamala Das, *My Story* (New Delhi: Sterling, 1977, 1998), 110.

21. See Kamala Das, 'The Fourteen Days' War', in *Wages of Love: Uncollected Writings of Kamala Das*, ed. Suresh Kohli (Noida: HarperCollins, 2013), 13.

22. The 2004 DC Books edition and the 2009 HarperCollins India edition.

23. Kamala Das, 'A Writer's Diary' (undated and unpublished typescript in the editor's collection), 2.

24. Ibid., 4.

25. Jaisurya Das, Quoted in Anjali Shetty, 'Writing Her Own Story', *DNA*, 23 February 2009, http://dnasyndication.com/showarticle.aspxnid=DNPUN12077 (accessed on 2 October 2014).

26. Kamala Das, 'A Writer's Diary' (undated and unpublished typescript in the editor's collection), 2.

27. Rukmini Bhaya Nair, 'For Kamala Das', *The Hyoid Bone* (New Delhi: Viking Penguin India, 1992), 24.

28. Malavika Sangghvi, 'Remembering Kamala', *Mid-Day*, posted 29 April 2013, http://www.mid-day.com/articles/words-of-wisdom/211048 (accessed on 9 August 2014).

29. Rita Karola Glass, *Meine Story* (Shokai, Osaka: Verlag Doilab, 1982).

30. Shailaja Ganguly, 'Kamala Das', *Femina* 25, no. 19 (October, 1984): 8–22.

31. Kamala Das, 'Obscenity and Literature', *Weekly Round Table* (23 April 1972): 31.

32. Letter to the editor.

33. Email to the editor, 4–5 June 2013.

34. Kamala Das, 'The First Meeting', *Collected Poems*, vol. I (Trivandrum: Navakerala Printers, 1984), 78.

35. Acceptance Speech at Sahitya Akademi Writers Meet, 25 February 1986; Kamala Das, *Wages of Love: Uncollected Writings of Kamala Das*, ed. Suresh Kohli (Noida: HarperCollins, 2013), 114.

36. 'Allah told me that in order to be effective, you should have political power.' Kamala Das, 'The Rediff Interview/Kamala Suraiya', interview with George Iype, Rediff.com, 19 July 2000, http://www.rediff.com/news/2000/jul/19inter.htm (accessed on 9 August 2014).

37. Kamala Das, 'I feel like P.T. Usha', interview with Ayyappa Prasad, *Sunday Observer*, 21 October 1984.

38. Pritam Sengupta et al., 'Top Quarks: Nobel Indians', *Outlook*, July 14 2003, http://www.outlookindia.com/article/Top-Quarks/220709 (accessed on 9 August 2014).

39. *Artes*: Tidskrift för Litteratur, Konstoch Musik, Svenska Akademien (Stockholm, The Royal Swedish Academy) no. 4 (July–August 1984): 67–76.

40. P.P. Raveendran, 'Text as History, History as Text: A Reading of Kamala Das's *Anamalai Poems*', in *Kamala Das: Critical Perspectives*, ed. Devindra Kohli (New Delhi: Pencraft International, 2010), 94–103.

41. Kamala Das, 'Summer Vacation', in *Contemporary Indian Short Stories*, eds Devindra Kohli and Barbara Schmidt-Haberkamp (Stuttgart: Reclam, 2006), 96–115.

42. Kamala Das, 'Of Masks and Memories: An Interview with Kamala Das', interview with P.P. Raveendran, *Indian Literature* XXXVI, no. 155 (May–June 1993): 148.

43. Kamala Das, 'running away from home', *Indian Literary Review* III, no. 3 (October 1985): 57–61, reprinted in *The Hindu*, 1 December 1996; reprinted as 'All the Lovers', in *Wages of Love: Uncollected Writings of Kamala Das*, ed. Suresh Kohli (Noida: HarperCollins, 2013), 21–29.

44. K. Satchidanandan, 'Obituary: Beyond the Body', *Frontline* 26, no. 13 (20 June–3 July 2009), http://www.hindu.com/thehindu/thscrip/print.pl?file=20090703261311400.htm&date=fl2613/&prd=fline&http://satchidanandan.blogspot.de/ (accessed on 9 August 2014).

45. Cited in 'Translators' Preface', in Kamala Das, *The Sandal Trees and Other Stories*, trans. from the Malayalam by V.C. Harris and C.K. Mohamed Ummer (Hyderabad: Disha Books, Orient Longman, 1995), vii.

46. Kamala Das, 'The Sparrow on the Glass-Pane', *Dialogue India 5, Indian Poetry Reivew*, ed. Pritish Nandy (Calcutta: Rina Nandy, Dialogue Publications, n.d.).

47. Jawaharlal Nehru quoted in 'Nehru—A Troubled Man', *Windsor Star*, 27 May 1964, 24, http://news.google.com/newspapers?id=tzA_AAAAIBAJ&sjid=81AMAAAAIBAJ&pg=4355,5162968&dq=kamala+nehru&hl=en (accessed on 9 August 2014).

48. Wayne Shumaker, *English Autobiography: Its Emergence, Materials, and Form* (Berkeley: University of California Press, 1954), 103.

49. Lynn Z. Bloom and Orlee Holder, 'Anais Nin's Diary in Context', *Mosaic* XI, no. 2 (Winter 1978), 193.

50. Eunice de Souza, *Talking Poems: Conversations with Poets* (New Delhi: Oxford University Press, 1999), 34.

51. Kamala Das, *A Childhood in Malabar: A Memoir*, trans. Gita Krishnakutty (New Delhi: Penguin India, 2003), 77.

51. Ibid., 203.

53. Kamala Das, *Encountering Kamala: Selections from the Poetry of Kamala Das*, with an Introduction by Andrew Arkin (New York: Gorgeous Notions Press, 2007), 49; Kamala Das and Suresh Kohli, *Closure: Some Poems and a Conversation* (Noida: HarperCollins, 2009), 15.

54. Susie Tharu and K. Lalita, eds, *Women's Writing in India: 600 B.C. to the Present*, vol. I (Delhi: Oxford University Press, 1991, 1993); Tharu and Lalita, 'Introduction', *Women's Writing in India*, vol. II, 7–8, 11.

55. Kamala Das, 'My Instinct, My Guru', in *Authors Speak*, ed. K. Satchidanandan (New Delhi: Sahitya Akademi, 2006), 136–37.

56. Kamala Das, 'Of Calcutta', *Collected Poems*, vol. I (Trivandrum: Navakerala Printers, 1984), 59.

57. Kamala Das quoted in facsimile, in 'Kamala Das as a Painter-Poet', PhD thesis, M.P. Devika, (Changanassery: S.B. College, Mahatma Gandhi University, 2001), 5–6, http://www.mgutheses.in/page/?q=T%20856&search=&page=&rad= (accessed on 10 August 2014).

58. Kamala Das, *My Story* (New Delhi: Sterling, 1977, 1998), 152.

59. Ibid.

60. Kamala Das, 'My Book of the Century', *Outlook*, 10 May 1999, http://www.outlookindia.com/article/My-Book-of-the-Century/207429 (accessed on 10 August 2014).

61. Arvind Krishna Mehrotra, annotation for 'Meera', in *Collected Poems of Arun Kolatkar*, ed. Arvind Krishna Mehrotra (Tarset, Northumberland: Bloodaxe Books, 2010), 368.

62. Kamala Das, 'Leaves of Grass on the Kerala Coast', *Span*: US Embassy magazine (October 1975): 30–31. Although she mentions 'the first edition', it could well have been a later edition since some of the poems she quotes from in her article did not appear in the first edition of *Leaves of Grass*.

63. Walt Whitman, 'Out of the Cradle Endlessly Rocking', 'Starting from Paumanok, 'By Broad Potomac's Shore', 'Faces', 'Song of the Redwood-Tree', 'This Compost' (first published in the 1867 edition), 'Bivouac on a Mountain Side', 'Crossing Brooklyn Ferry', 'Night on the Prairies' (1860), 'Song of the Broad-Axe', 'Poets to Come' and 'Pioneers! O Pioneers!'.

64. Alicia Ostriker, 'Loving Walt Whitman and the Problem of America', in *The Continuing Presence of Walt Whitman*, ed. Robert K. Martin (Iowa City: Iowa University Press, 1992), 217–32.

65. Kamala Das, 'Answers to a Questionnaire', interview with Subhas C. Saha, *Insights* (Calcutta: Writers Workshop, 1972): 15.

66. Kamala Das in *Kamala Das: An Introduction* (a Sahitya Akademi documentary film), dir. Suresh Kohli; Kamala Das quoted in Suresh Kohli, 'Still a Rebel Writer: Writer and Poet Kamala Das on Her Works and Why She Writes', *The Hindu*, 13 August 2006, http://www.hindu.com/mag/2006 /08/13/stories/2006081300080500.htm (accessed on 16 August 2006), and in Kamala Das and Suresh Kohli, *Closure: Some Poems and a Conversation* (Noida: HarperCollins, 2009), 74.

67. Kamala Das, 'Dedication', in *Encountering Kamala: Selections from the Poetry of Kamala Das*, with an Introduction by Andrew Arkin (New York: Gorgeous Notions Press, 2007).

68. Kamala Das quoted in 'Kamala Das as a Painter-Poet', PhD thesis, M.P. Devika, (Changanassery: S.B. College, Mahatma Gandhi University, 2001), 154, 216, http://www.mgutheses.in/page/?q=T%20856&search=&page=&rad= (accessed on 10 August 2014).

69. Ibid.

70. Kamala Das, 'I Believe', *Savvy*, December 1990.

71. Besides drawing six sketches, Kamala Das also typed in verse

lines on twenty-three different pages, corrected or completed some of these by hand, and signed with a note, dated 23 July 1978.

72. Elaine Hedges and Ingrid Wendt, eds, *Her Own Image: Women Working in the Arts* (New York: Feminist Press, 1980), 151–55.

73. Kamala Das quoted in 'Kamala Das as a Painter-Poet', PhD thesis, M.P. Devika, (Changanassery: S.B. College, Mahatma Gandhi University, 2001), 230–31, http://www.mgutheses.in/page/?q=T%20856&search=&page=&rad= (accessed on 10 August 2014).

74. Ibid.

75. Alice Walker, 'Be Nobody's Darling', *Revolutionary Petunias and Other Poems* (New York and London: Harcourt Brace, 1971, 1972, 1973), 31–32.

76. David McCutchion, *Indian Writing in English: Critical Essays* (Calcutta: Writers Workshop, 1969, 1973), 135, 142.

77. Carol Rumens, 'Dislocated Sensibility', *Poetry Review* (Spring 1993); reprinted in *Kamala Das: Critical Perspectives*, ed. Devindra Kohli (New Delhi: Pencraft International 2010), 114–16.

78. Chris Wallace-Crabbe, 'The Loud Posters of Kamala Das', *Kamala Das: A Selection with Essays on Her Work*', eds S.C. Harrex and Vincent O'Sullivan (Adelaide: Centre for Research in the New Literatures in English, 1986), 217–23; reprinted in *Kamala Das: Critical Perspectives*, ed. Devindra Kohli (New Delhi: Pencraft International 2010), 159–65.

79. '"The 'Tongue in English Chains": Indo-English Poetry Today", in *Indian Poetry in English: Essays in Criticism*, eds V.A. Shahane and M. Sivaramakrishna (Hyderabad: Osmania University, 1977), 240.

80. Kamala Das, *The Sandal Trees and Other Stories*, trans. from the Malayalam by V.C. Harris and C.K. Mohamed Ummer, (Hyderabad: Disha Books, Orient Longman, 1995), 26. Towards the end of the short story 'The Sandal Trees', when the husband confronts his wife with her lingering but unacknowledged love for Kalaynikutty, who had made lesbian overtures to her in adolescence, as the real cause of their failed marriage, he ruefully remarks: 'I was a mere drizzle arriving hesitantly, timidly, after a full storm.'

81. Rosemary Marangoly George, 'Calling Kamala Das Queer: Rereading "My Story"', *Feminist Studies* 26, no. 3 (Autumn 2000): 750.

82. Kamala Das quoted in 'Kamala Das as a Painter-Poet', PhD thesis, M.P. Devika, (Changanassery: S.B. College, Mahatma Gandhi University, 2001), 233, http://www.mgutheses.in/page/?q=T%20856&search=&page=&rad= (accessed on 10 August 2014).

83. Robert Graves, *The White Goddess* (London: Faber, 1948), 449.

84. Ibid., 447.

85. Rukmini Bhaya Nair, 'The Testament of the Tenth Muse: Toward a Feminist Sensibility', in *Lying on the Postcolonial Couch: The Idea of Indifference* (Minneapolis and London: University of Minnesota Press, 2002), 222.

86. Bruce King, *Modern Indian Poetry in English* (New Delhi: Oxford University Press, 2005), 135, 142.

87. Kamala Das quoted in Merrily Weisbord, *The Love Queen of Malabar: Memoir of a Friendship with Kamala Das* (Gurgaon: Research Press, 2011), 62.

88. Jaisurya Das, 'Thus Spake Das', interview with Sangeeta Barooah Pisharoty, *The Hindu*, October 21 2010, www.thehindu.com/todays-paper/tp-features/tp-metroplus/thus-spake-das/article853590.ece (accessed on 10 August 2014).

89. M.D. Nalapat, 'Interview with M.D. Nalapat', *twocircles TV*, YouTube.com, uploaded July 21 2009, https://www.youtube.com/watch?v=cMdGvF8bPgQ (accessed on 5 October 2014).

90. Kamala Das, *Wages of Love: Uncollected Writings of Kamala Das*, ed. Suresh Kohli (Noida: HarperCollins, 2013), 163.

91. Jeet Thayil, 'The Reckoning', *Caravan*, 1 May 2010, www.caravanmagazine.in/fiction-poetry/reckoning (accessed on 10 August 2014).

92. Kamala Das, 'Noose', in *Wages of Love: Uncollected Writings of Kamala Das*, ed. Suresh Kohli (Noida: HarperCollins, 2013), 148.

Poems

From *Summer in Calcutta* (1965)

An Introduction

I don't know politics but I know the names
Of those in power, and can repeat them like
Days of week, or names of months, beginning with
Nehru. I am Indian, very brown, born in
Malabar, I speak three languages, write in
Two, dream in one. Don't write in English, they said,
English is not your mother-tongue. Why not leave
Me alone, critics, friends, visiting cousins,
Every one of you? Why not let me speak in
Any language I like? The language I speak
Becomes mine, its distortions, its queernesses
All mine, mine alone. It is half English, half
Indian, funny perhaps, but it is honest,
It is as human as I am human, don't
You see? It voices my joys, my longings, my
Hopes, and it is useful to me as cawing
Is to crows or roaring to the lions, it
Is human speech, the speech of the mind that is
Here and not there, a mind that sees and hears and
Is aware. Not the deaf, blind speech
Of trees in storm or of monsoon clouds or of rain or th
Incoherent mutterings of the blazing
Funeral pyre. I was child, and later they
Told me I grew, for I became tall, my limbs
Swelled and one or two places sprouted hair. When
I asked for love, not knowing what else to ask
For, he drew a youth of sixteen into the
Bedroom and closed the door. He did not beat me
But my sad woman-body felt so beaten.

The weight of my breasts and womb crushed me. I shrank
Pitifully. Then . . . I wore a shirt and my
Brother's trousers, cut my hair short and ignored
My womanliness. Dress in sarees, be girl,
Be wife, they said. Be embroiderer, be cook,
Be a quarreller with servants. Fit in. Oh,
Belong, cried the categorizers. Don't sit
On walls or peep in through our lace-draped windows.

Be Amy, or be Kamala. Or, better
Still, be Madhavikutty. It is time to
Choose a name, a role. Don't play pretending games.
Don't play at schizophrenia or be a
Nympho. Don't cry embarrassingly loud when
Jilted in love . . . I met a man, loved him. Call
Him not by any name, he is every man
Who wants woman, just as I am every
Woman who seeks love. In him . . . the hungry haste
Of rivers, in me . . . the ocean's tireless
Waiting. Who are you, I ask each and every one,
The answer is, it is I. Anywhere and
Everywhere, I see the one who calls himself
I; in this world, he is tightly packed like the
Sword in its sheath. It is I who drink lonely
Drinks at twelve, midnight, in hotels of strange towns,
It is I who laugh, it is I who make love
And then, feel shame, it is I who lie dying
With a rattle in my throat. I am sinner,
I am saint. I am the beloved and the
Betrayed. I have no joys which are not yours, no
Aches which are not yours. I too call myself I.

The Dance of the Eunuchs

It was hot, so hot, before the eunuchs came
To dance, wide skirts going round and round, cymbals
Richly clashing, and anklets jingling, jingling,
Jingling . . . Beneath the fiery gulmohur, with
Long braids flying, dark eyes flashing, they danced and
They danced, oh, they danced till they bled . . . There were green
Tattoos on their cheeks, jasmines in their hair, some
Were dark and some were almost fair. Their voices
Were harsh, their songs melancholy; they sang of
Lovers dying and of children left unborn . . .
Some beat their drums; others beat their sorry breasts
And wailed, and writhed in vacant ecstasy. They
Were thin in limbs and dry, like half-burnt logs from
Funeral pyres, a drought and a rottenness
Were in each of them. Even the crows were so
Silent on trees, and the children, wide eyed, still;
All were watching these poor creatures' convulsions.
The sky crackled then, thunder came, and lightning
And rain, a meagre rain that smelt of dust in
Attics and the urine of lizards and mice . . .

Pigeons

Pigeons on the ledge
Of an afternoon dream
Sit strangely silent,
The hot dust rises,
Falls on sun-peeled beaks;
On a city of fevered
Lanes.
The sun swells; then
Swollen like a fruit
It runs harsh silver threads
Lengthwise, my afternoon
Dream.

The Freaks

He talks, turning a sun-stained
Cheek to me, his mouth, a dark
Cavern, where stalactites of
Uneven teeth gleam, his right
Hand on my knee, while our minds
Are willed to race towards love;
But, they only wander, tripping
Idly over puddles of
Desire . . . Can this man with
Nimble finger-tips unleash
Nothing more alive than the
Skin's lazy hungers? Who can
Help us who have lived so long
And have failed in love? The heart,
An empty cistern, waiting
Through long hours, fills itself
With coiling snakes of silence.
I am a freak. It's only
To save my face, I flaunt, at
Times, a grand, flamboyant lust.

Words

All round me are words, and words and words,
They grow on me like leaves, they never
Seem to stop their slow growing
From within . . . But I tell myself, words
Are a nuisance, beware of them, they
Can be so many things, a
Chasm where running feet must pause, to
Look, a sea with paralysing waves,
A blast of burning air or,
A knife most willing to cut your best
Friend's throat . . . Words are a nuisance, but
They grow on me like leaves on a tree,
They never seem to stop their coming
From a silence, somewhere deep within . . .

In Love

Of what does the burning mouth
Of sun, burning in today's
Sky remind me oh, yes, his
Mouth . . . and his limbs like pale and
Carnivorous plants reaching
Out for me, and the sad lie
Of my unending lust. Where
Is room, excuse or even
Need for love, for, isn't each
Embrace a complete thing,
A finished jigsaw, when mouth on
Mouth, I lie, ignoring my poor
Moody mind, while pleasure
With deliberate gaiety
Trumpets harshly into the
Silence of the room . . . At noon
I watch sleek crows flying
Like poison on wings - and at
Night, from behind the Burdwan
Road, the corpse-bearers cry 'Bol
Hari Bol', a strange lacing
For moonless nights, while I walk
The verandah, sleepless,
A million questions awake in
Me, and all about him, and
This skin-communicated
Thing that I dare not yet in
His presence call our love.

The Fear of the Year

This is no age for slow desires,
Desired on lengths of idle beds
Beside indifferent faces,
For no smile, however fond, can
Settle time like a paper weight.
That time survives and moves beyond
This moment's diminutive pride
Is itself an incredible
Thing; for fear has warped us all; even
In the freedom of our dreams, it
Thrusts its paws to incarnadine
The virgin whiteness, so that we
Perceive the flying steel hands sow
Over mellow cities those dark,
Malevolent seeds and the red,
Red, mushrooms hotly sprout and grow
On an earth illogically
Stilled, and silenced, and dead, dead, dead.

My Grandmother's House

There is a house now far away where once
I received love . . . That woman died,
The house withdrew into silence, snakes moved
Among books I was then too young
To read, and, my blood turned cold like the moon.
How often I think of going
There, to peer through blind eyes of windows or
Just listen to the frozen air,
Or in wild despair, pick an armful of
Darkness to bring it here to lie
Behind my bedroom door like a brooding
Dog . . . you cannot believe, darling,
Can you, that I lived in such a house and
Was proud, and loved . . . I who have lost
My way and beg now at strangers' doors to
Receive love, at least in small change?

A Relationship

This love, older than I by myriad
Saddened centuries, was once a prayer
In his bones that made them grow in years of
Adolescence to this favoured height; yes,
It was my desire that made him male
And beautiful, so that when at last we
Met, to believe that once I knew not his
Form, his quiet touch, or the blind kindness
Of his lips was hard indeed. Betray me?
Yes, he can, but never physically;
Only with words that curl their limbs at
Touch of air and die with metallic sighs.
What care I for their quick, sterile sting, while
My body's wisdom tells and tells again
That I shall find my rest, my sleep, my peace
And even death nowhere else but here in
My betrayer's arm . . .

Radha Krishna

This becomes from this hour
Our river and this old Kadamba
Tree, ours alone, for our homeless
Souls to return someday
To hang like bats from its pure
Physicality . . . .

The End of Spring

While I wait for your phone call, I do not
Know who to believe. You, who say you love,
Or the voice that tells me no, no, no . . .
Split each minute into strangers, a lot
Of them, a sort of game to fill the void
In time, and avoid owning up to old
Deceits. The street outside is dark and moist
Like limbs of sleeping girls. The lights go out
And night begins, a change of colour, what
Else? So might my senses fail and death like
Night arrive. I journey while alone just
Backwards, taking secret steps inwards and
Choosing roads none has walked before. My fear
Is the fear of change; re-assuring me,
As you do so often, does not help, for
Even blood gets a colour-change, exposed.

The spring dehydrating like a grape, meek
Cow-smells on the breath of winds, and your voice,
Now on the telephone . . . What is the use
Of love, all this love, if all it gives is
Fear, you the fear of storms asleep in you,
And me the fear of hurting you?

Loud Posters

I am today a creature turned inside
Out. To spread myself across wide highways
Of your thoughts, stranger, like a loud poster
Was always my desire, but all I
Do is lurk in shadows of culs-de-sac,
Just two eyes showing . . . oh, never mind, I've
Spent long years trying to locate my mind
Beneath skin, beneath flesh and underneath
The bone. I've stretched my two-dimensional
Nudity on sheets of weeklies, monthlies,
Quarterlies, a sad sacrifice. I've put
My private voice away, adopted the
Typewriter's click as my only speech; I
Click-click, click-click tiresomely into your
Ears, stranger, though you may have no need of
Me, I go on and on, not knowing why . . .

Farewell to Bombay

I take leave of you, fair city, while tears
Hide somewhere in my adult eyes
And sadness is silent as a stone
In the river's unmoving
Core . . .
It's goodbye, goodbye, goodbye
To slender shapes behind window panes
Shut against indiscriminate desire
And rain; to yellow moons
So long ignored, so long unloved;
To the birds, flesh-hungry,
Circling in the sky
With shrill and hostile cries; to the crowd
Near the sea, walking or sitting
But always talking, talking,
Talking . . .
I take leave of you, fair city, keep your tears,
Your anger and your smile for others,
Young, who come with unjaded eyes;
Give them your sad-eyed courtesans with tinsel
And jasmine in their hair, your marble
Slabs in morgues, your brittle
Roadside laughter . . .
It's goodbye, goodbye, goodbye . . .
To the silence and the sounds;
To streets that I never walked
But in dreams, to lips that I never kissed
But in dreams; to children
Lovely as flowers, out of me
Never born . . .

My Morning Tree

Dear tree, ugly tree, I call you my morning
Tree, and when I wake, I run to look at you . . .
No leaves, no buds, no flowers, just your branches
Like dry roots stretching towards the unfertile
Sky. An old hag's fleshless limbs, a hand thrown up
In despair; no hope, no hope, no hope at all . . .

On some days, the mist's gossamer drapes your limbs . . .
Or, the dusky buzzards crouch on them with quiet
Feathers, like sinister fruits and I wonder
If they will swell and ripen too, and the juice
Ooze out on to your passive limbs, your passive
Trunk, the warm blood trickling, trickling, trickling . . .

Morning tree, on your brown bony branch, one day,
I shall see a sudden flower, and know at once
That my death is just a flower, a red, red,
Morning flower, and then, from behind the cold
Window-pane, I shall smile my last morning's smile . . .

Someone Else's Song

I am a million, million people
Talking all at once, with voices
Raised in clamour, like maids
At village-wells.

I am a million, million deaths
Pox-clustered, each a drying seed
Someday to be shed, to grow for
Someone else, a memory.

I am a million, million births
Flushed with triumphant blood, each a growing
Thing that thrusts its long-nailed hands
To scar the hollow air.

I am a million, million silences
Strung like crystal beads
Onto someone else's
Song.

The Stranger and I

Stranger with despair in your eyes
I've met you not here alone, but
In alien towns, where even the streets
You walked on, looking, no, not at
Faces, but at signs over shops, were
Roofed with hostile skies; everything
Seemed so grey, so old, but you walked
On and on, your fingers in pockets
Curling and uncurling, your loneliness
Blue as a birthmark on your face . . .

I've seen you in restaurants, all gay
And smoke-filled, on the seat behind
The pillar, drinking joylessly your
Sweetened tea, while your left hand
Softly trembling, crouches on the
Tablecloth like a wounded bird . . .

I've seen you walk around in gardens
Pausing to peer at names, knife-engraved
On trees now grown tall; on beaches,
With downcast eyes, at cocktails,
Glass in hand, sulking behind those
Potted plants; I've seen your bitten nails,
Your sickly smile, heard your brittle
Broken talk; I know you now too well
Not to recognise . . .

A Hot Noon in Malabar

This is a noon for beggars with whining
Voices, a noon for men who come from hills
With parrots in a cage and fortune-cards,
All stained with time, for brown Kurava girls
With old eyes, who read palms in light singsong
Voices, for bangle-sellers who spread
On the cool black floor those red and green and blue
Bangles, all covered with the dust of roads,
For all of them, whose feet, devouring rough
Miles, grow cracks on the heels, so that when they
Clambered up our porch, the noise was grating,
Strange . . . This is a noon for strangers who part
The window-drapes and peer in, their hot eyes
Brimming with the sun, not seeing a thing in
Shadowy rooms and turn away and look
So yearningly at the brick-ledged well. This
Is a noon for strangers with mistrust in
Their eyes, dark, silent ones who rarely speak
At all, so that when they speak, their voices
Run wild, like jungle-voices. Yes, this is
A noon for wild men, wild thoughts, wild love. To
Be here, far away, is torture. Wild feet
Stirring up the dust, this hot noon, at my
Home in Malabar, and I so far away . . .

The Sunshine Cat

They did this to her, the men who knew her, the man
She loved, who loved her not enough, being selfish
And a coward, the husband who neither loved nor
Used her, but was a ruthless watcher, and the band
Of cynics she turned to, clinging to their chests where
New hair sprouted like great-winged moths, burrowing her
Face into their smells and their young lusts to forget,
To forget, oh, to forget . . . and, they said, each of
Them, I do not love, I cannot love, it is not
In my nature to love, but I can be kind to you . . .
They let her slide from pegs of sanity into
A bed made soft with tears and she lay there weeping,
For sleep had lost its use; I shall build walls with tears,
She said, walls to shut me in . . . Her husband shut her
In, every morning; locked her in a room of books
With a streak of sunshine lying near the door, like
A yellow cat, to keep her company, but soon,
Winter came and one day while locking her in, he
Noticed that the cat of sunshine was only a
Line, a hair-thin line, and in the evening when
He returned to take her out, she was a cold and
Half-dead woman, now of no use at all to men.

Forest Fire

Of late I have begun to feel a hunger
To take in with greed, like a forest fire that
Consumes, and, with each killing gains a wilder,
Brighter charm, all that comes my way. Bald child in
Open pram, you think I only look, and you
Too, slim lovers behind the tree and you, old
Man with paper in your hand and sunlight in
Your hair . . . My eyes lick at you like flames, my nerves
Consume; and, when I finish with you, in the
Pram, near the tree and, on the park bench, I spit
Out small heaps of ash, nothing else. But in me
The sights and smells and sounds shall thrive and go on
And on and on. In me shall sleep the baby
That sat in prams, and, sleep and wake and smile its
Toothless smile. In me shall walk the lovers, hand
In hand, and in me, where else, the old shall sit
And feel the touch of sun. In me, the street-lamps
Shall glimmer, the cabaret girls cavort, the
Wedding drums resound, the eunuchs swirl coloured
Skirts and sing sad songs of love, the wounded moan,
And in me the dying mother with hopeful
Eyes shall gaze around, seeking her child, now grown
And gone away to other towns, other arms.

I Shall Some Day

I shall some day leave, leave the cocoon
You built around me with morning tea,
Love-words flung from doorways and of course
Your tired lust. I shall someday take
Wings, fly around, as often petals
Do when free in air, and you dear one,
Just the sad remnant of a root, must
Lie behind, sans pride, on double-beds
And grieve. But, I shall someday return, losing
Nearly all, hurt by wind, sun and rain,
Too hurt by fierce happiness to want
A further jaunt or a further spell
Of freedom, and I shall someday see
My world, de-fleshed, de-veined, de-blooded,
Just a skeletal thing, then shut my
Eyes and take refuge, if nowhere else,
Here in your nest of familiar scorn . . .

Summer in Calcutta

What is this drink but
The April sun, squeezed
Like an orange in
My glass? I sip the
Fire, I drink and drink
Again, I am drunk,
Yes, but on the gold
Of suns. What noble
Venom now flows through
My veins and fills my
Mind with unhurried
Laughter? My worries
Doze. Wee bubbles ring
My glass, like a bride's
Nervous smile, and meet
My lips. Dear, forgive
This moment's lull in
Wanting you, the blur
In memory. How
Brief the term of my
Devotion, how brief
Your reign when I with
Glass in hand, drink, drink,
And drink again this
Juice of April suns.

Afterwards

Son of my womb,
Ugly in loneliness,
You walk the world's bleary eye
Like grit. Your cleverness
Shall not be your doom
As ours was. I will tell you why.

Just a while ago, this place
Was ours. You should have seen us race
Thread-wise across this turquoise sky
And talk of love, music, science
And beauty. Lovers held hands

And watched the eagles fly
Too near the sun and fall,
Children were told not to lie
And it was normal for a girl to sigh
Over a dying bird; we learnt kindness
As we learnt our books, yes.

There was no sign at all of what was
Coming then, the earth was
Sagging heavy, fruits were sweet
And ripe, fishes died on their bait,
And as a little girl, I watched
My brothers squat beside a hedge
And slowly blind a beetle.
The thorny twig in those little
Hands went quickly red-tipped.
The insect curled its legs and died.

I felt sad, but my tears I tried to hide.
That was what I was, your mother.

Son. You turn round in another
Yellow disc of light, as I did
In mine, once. They ask me
Is this the one we died for? we?
We who made gigantic dreams
Of peace. We who had whims

And fancies fit for gods, we
Set the poison to our lips, content to be
Curers, we judged the sinners
And killed them; but let that be.
What are you, with vacuum in your mind
Too dry for growth, just a rind we left behind.

With no memory to kindle sadness
In your eyes, no dream of feminine smiles
To excite your open-mouthed sleep.
From us to you was a gigantic leap.

The earth we nearly killed is yours
Now. The flowers bloom again,
But a savage red; it takes
Time to forget blood or the quick gasps
Of the dying. And the sudden pain,
But the sun came again, and rain.

You have to be happy now,
Learn to do without love,
It's easier when alone, go ahead,
There is no song to break your
Somnambulistic tread.
Caught in this yellow disc of light,
You turn, like a guilty rat
And draw your rocky home over you
Like an irremovable shell.
The dead do not understand your
Desire to be alone, but every hour
Of your life is yours, do not worry.

They watch and speak in jealousy
But not I. While I was young
From every living moment I wrung
Only tears, I was restless,
My thoughts knew no lull, as tides
That never shrank or grew.

Even fowls had their one-legged
Sleep. Not I. How fervently I wished
That I could send those moods flying,
Away like sun-blinded bats
To resume their silent hanging
In other alcoves, not mine.

For me, there was no change
In the harsh yellow moon,
No peace, no goal at all in eye's range.
Life lay huddled in prisoner's robes
Waiting for easy extinction.
I sat in a gallery seat and looked
Till my insomniac eyes ached
But that was how I grew. Growth was
Definiteness, the much-ironed folds
Of a school uniform;
A man who let me take his name
To make me feel I belonged.

You, son, walking in loneliness
Now, hairless, blank-faced, looking
For the key your fathers lost,
Take heart, just a while ago
Your mother groaned in labour pain
And slept; and then your first cry rose
To stun the silence of her dreams.

The Siesta

Sleep to her was the sun-lit tank
Her girl-thin limbs played in.
Turtles moved in its hostile depths, dank,
Dusky eels stared with opal eyes, but
In all those unfenced hours, she had felt
No fear, nor even joy, but
An anonymous peace.
The dreams glow pearl-white, to her,
They seem hardly mortal.
But as evening comes,
Snake-like, she sheds
Their silver coils and wakes
To meet this alien world which talks
Of Gods and casual sins.
Has she the courage, the sense
To pick herself an average
Identity, to age
Through years of earthy din
Gently, like a cut flower until
It's time to be removed; or, will she
Wander,
Fog-eyed, seeking another
To be hers, her own to love
Or destroy; to share with her
The dim-lit gloom where
She moves like a fawn?

The Testing of the Sirens

The night, black-cloaked like a procuress, brought
him to me, willing, light as a shadow,
speaking words of love
in some tender language I do not know . . .

With the crows came the morning, and my limbs
warm of love, were once again so lonely . . .

At my doorstep I saw a pock-marked face,
a friendly smile and
a rolleiflex. We will go for a drive,
he said. Or, go to see the lakes. I have
washed my face with soap and water, brushed
my hair a dozen
times, draped myself in six yards of printed
voile. Ah . . . does it still show, my night of love?

You look pale, he said. Not pale, not really
pale. It's the lipstick's
anaemia. Out in the street, we heard
the sirens go, and I paused in talk to
weave their wail with the sound of his mirthless
laughter. He said,
they are testing the sirens today. I am
happy. He really was lavish with words.
I'm happy, just being with you. But you . . .
you love another,
I know, he said, perhaps a handsome man,
A young and handsome man. Not young,
not handsome, I thought, just a filthy snob.

It's a one-sided love,
I said. What can I do for you? I smiled.
A smile is such a detached thing, I wear
it like a flower. Near the lake, a pregnant
girl bared her dusky
breasts and washed them sullenly. On the old
cannon-stand, crows bickered over a piece
of lizard-meat and the white sun was there
and everywhere . . .

I want your photo, lying down, he said,
against those rusty nineteen-thirty-four guns,
will you? Sure. Just arrange my limbs and tell
me when to smile. I
shut my eyes, but inside eye-lids, there was
no more light, no more love, or peace, only
the white, white sun burning, burning, burning . . .

Ah, why does love come to me like pain
again and again and again?

With Its Quiet Tongue

My heart—the wretched thing—is today
Cold, like those pale green mirrors
One sees in corridors . . .

They looked in with timid eyes, hungry
Perhaps for flattery, and smiled
Their happiest smiles before they
Walked away . . .

They left the mirror cold, and so
Beautiful; how much kinder to have
Left a great, sprawling crack, shaped
Like a spider's web . . .

But why cry? or, why even gloat
In solitude? What does a woman lose
Or even gain from a love-affair?
The passions' dying is not a death
At all but a sleep . . .

The night-wind walks my street
Tap-tapping, like a blinded
Man; its grief overcomes me; I crave
At this hour, not for faces that I knew
Or for the voices that I loved but
For sleep—a sleep which has like an Indian
Bride, proud loveless eyes
And a quiet tongue.

The Wild Bougainvillea

There was a time when I
Was sad in Calcutta, a few summer days
That passed slowly, and
Moodily, like the mourners behind a bier. Days
When even my bed gave
No rest, but like a troubled sea, tossed me on
Its waves, and how I groaned
And moaned, and constantly yearned for a man from
Another town . . . Then, by
And by, my love wilted, for I took long walks,
Walked roads I had never
Seen before, saw faces I liked for their charm.
It is a good world, and
Packed with distractions. I walked through streets beside
The sea, where the barges
Float, their undersides rotting and the garbage
Rot, and the dead fish rot,
And, I smelt the smell of dying things and the
Heavy smell of rotting
Dead, I walked on streets where the night-girls with sham
Obtrusive breasts sauntered
And under yellow lamps, up-and-down wandered
Beaming their sickly smiles
At men. And, on streets near old cemeteries
Where the dead are so dead
That even their tombstones have lost their names in
The rains, and are pale now
And yellowed like grotesque teeth—a harvest of
Old teeth—and no mourner
Ever sheds a bouquet for them or a tear

But, I did see beside
The olden tombs some marigolds bloom and the
Wild red bougainvillea
Climbing their minarets. I walked, I saw and
I heard, the city tamed
Itself for me, and then my hunger for a
Particular touch waned
And one day I sent him some roses and slept
Through the night, a silent
Dreamless sleep and woke up in the morning, free.

From *The Descendants* (1967)

The Suicide

Bereft of soul
my body shall be bare.
Bereft of body
my soul shall be bare.

Which would you rather have
O kind sea?
which is the more dead
of the two?

I throw the bodies out,
I cannot stand their smell.
Only the souls may enter
The vortex of the sea.
Only the souls know how to sing
At the vortex of the sea.

Your body shall be dead,
Poor thing,
Dead as driftwood, drifting
And drifting to the shore.
Your body shall ride the tide,
Rider, slumped dead
On white war-horse,
Charging.

Your body shall bruise white
against the coral reefs,
your body,
your lonely body.

I tell you, sea,
I have enough courage to die,
But not enough.
Not enough to disobey him
Who said: Do not die
And hurt me that certain way.

How easy your duties are.
How simple.
Only roar a hungry roar,
Leap forward,
And retreat.

You swing and you swing,
O sea, you play a child's game.

But,
I must pose,
I must pretend,
I must act the role
Of happy woman,
Happy wife.
I must keep the right distance
Between me and the high.
I must keep the right distance
Between me and the low.

O sea, I am fed up
I want to be simple
I want to be loved
And
If love is not to be had,
I want to be dead . . .

While I enter deeper,
With joy I discover
The sea's hostile cold
Is after all skin-deep.
The sea's inner chambers
are all very warm.
There must be a sun slumbering
At the vortex of the sea.

O sea, I am happy swimming
Happy, happy, happy . . .
The only movement I know well
Is certainly the swim.
It comes naturally to me.
I had a house in Malabar
and a pale-green pond.
I did all my growing there
In the bright summer months.
I swam about and floated,
I lay speckled green and gold
In all the hours of the sun,
Until
My grandmother cried,
Darling, you must stop this bathing now.
You are much too big to play
Naked in the pond.

Yes, the only movement I really know
Is swimming,
It comes naturally to me.
The white man who offers
To help me forget,

The white man who offers
Himself as a stiff drink,
Is for me,
To tell the truth,
Only water.
Only a pale-green pond
Glimmering in the sun.
In him I swim
All broken with longing.
In his robust blood I float
Drying off my tears.

Yet I never can forget
The only man who hurts.
The only one who seems to know
The only way to hurt.

Holding you is easy
Clutching at moving water,
I tell you, sea,
This is easy.
But to hold him for half a day
Was a difficult task.
It required drinks
To hold him down.
To make him love.
But, when he did love,
Believe me,
All I could do was sob like a fool.

O sea,
You generous cow,
You and I are big flops.
We are too sentimental
For our own
Good.

Lights are moving on the shore.
But I shall not return.

Sea, toss my body back
That he knew how to love.

Bereft of body
My soul shall be free.

Take in my naked soul
That he knew how to hurt.

Only the soul knows how to sing
At the vortex of the sea.

The Descendants

We have spent our youth in gentle sinning
Exchanging some insubstantial love and
Often thought we were hurt, but no pain in
Us could remain, no bruise could scar or
Even slightly mar our cold loveliness.
We have lain in every weather, nailed, no, not
To crosses, but to soft beds and against
Softer forms, while the heaving, lurching,
Tender hours passed in a half-dusk, half-dawn and
Half-dream, half-real trance. We were the yielders,
Yielding ourselves to everything. It is
Not for us to scrape the walls of wombs for
Memories, not for us even to
Question death, but as child to mother's arms
We shall give ourselves to the fire or to
The hungry earth to be slowly eaten,
Devoured. None will step off his cross
Or show his wounds to us, no god lost in
Silence shall begin to speak, no lost love
Claim us, no, we are not going to be
Ever redeemed, or made new.

Radha

The long waiting
Had made their bond so chaste, and all the doubting

And the reasoning
So that in his first true embrace, she was girl

And virgin crying
Everything in me
Is melting, even the hardness at the core
O Krishna, I am melting, melting, melting

Nothing remains but
You . . .

Palam

Like blood running out and death beginning,
Another day is ending, while planes drone on
In the distance and the airport lights gleam blue.
Do not turn a blurry face towards me this time or wave
But let evening swallow all I loved this humbled afternoon.
Go deep into night, a victor as cold now as his blade,
Dark falcon, late returning.
Walk away from me into the lonely night
With my finger-prints on you, my darling, go,
While like blood running out and death beginning,
This day of ours is helplessly ending.

Luminol

Love-lorn,
It is only
Wise at times, to let sleep
Make holes in memory, even
If it
Be the cold and
Luminous sleep banked in
The heart of pills, for he shall not
Enter,
Your ruthless one,
Being human, clumsy
With noise and movement, the soul's mute
Arena,
That silent sleep inside your sleep.

Substitute

Memory
Great moody sea,
Do not thump so
Against my shore.

Let me lie still
Without thought or will.
For a benign hour or two,
Dear night, be my tomb.

It is hard to believe
That I only lost,
Lost all, lost even
What I never had.

Life is quite simple now—
Love, blackmail and sorrow.

It will be all right when I learn
To paint my mouth like a clown's.
It will be all right if I put up my hair,
Stand near my husband to make a proud pair.

It will be all right if I join clubs
And flirt a little over telephone.
It will be all right, it will be all right
I am the type that endures.

It will be all right, it will be all right
It will be all right between the world and me.

It will be all right if I don't remember
The last of the days together . . .

. . . Over market-square the poor crows
With raucous cries flailed the sky.
Our bodies after love-making
Turned away, rejecting.
Our words began to sound
Like clatter of swords in fight.

Yet, I was thinking, lying beside him
That I loved, and was much loved.
It is a physical thing, he said suddenly,
End it, I cried, end it, and let us be free.

This freedom was our last strange toy.
Like the hangman's robe, even while new
It could give no pride. Nor even joy.
We kissed and we loved, all in a fury,
For another short hour or two
We went all warm and wild and lovely.

After that love became a swivel-door,
When one went out, another came in.

Then I lost count, for always in my arms
Was a substitute for a substitute.
Oh, what is the use, explaining—
It was a nameless, faceless crowd.

All I remember is the first beautiful face
All I want to forget is that beautiful face.
It will be all right if I don't remember
The last of the days together.

It will be all right, it will be all right
It will be all right between the world and me.

Ferns

Certain it is that a time will come when
One of us will cry, candle, burn no more
At both ends burn dimly now, and feet that have
So long but rambled will then break into
A run, recognising for the first time
The pale street's horror, and run with the wind
To seek for warm hollows where human sounds
Never echoed, seas that whip the craggy
Shores and mountains where darkness grows like ferns,
To hide, to hide and save what remains of
Pride. Certain it is that a time will come
When words, while uttered, will fall thudding down
Like dismembered heads and love will ride damp
Night-streets grinning in static mirth and at
Quiet places eat its own hotted flesh
And wait for it to grow again, and our
Bodies stacked on beds will mimic the slow
Gestures of the mind and take on the blame
In silent sin. Escape now from such bonds
And from the precious staleness that we drag
From one country to another, waiting
Patiently at counters, evading no
Law, and which to willing arms are thrust with
A sigh and "I've waited so long for you".

The Maggots

At sunset, on the river bank, Krishna
Loved her for the last time and left.
That night in her husband's arms, Radha felt
So dead that he asked, what is wrong,
Do you mind my kisses, love? and she said,
No, not at all, but thought, what is
It to the corpse if the maggots nip?

Annette

Annette,
At the dresser.
Pale fingers over mirror-fields
Reaping
That wheat brown hair.
Beauty
Falling as chaff in old mirrors,
While calendars
In all
The cities turn . . .

The Doubt

When a man is dead, or a woman,
We call the corpse not he
Or she but it. Does it
Not mean that we believe
That only the souls have sex and that
Sex is invisible?
Then the question is, who
Is the man, who the girl,
All sex-accessories being no
Indication. Is she
A male who with frail hands
Clasps me to her breast, while
The silence in her sickroom, turning
Eloquent, accuses
Me of ingratitude?
And, is he female who
After love, smoothes out the bed sheets with
Finicky hands and plucks
From pillows strands of hair?
. . . How well I can see him
After a murder, conscientiously
Tidy up the scene, wash
The bloodstains under the
Faucet, bury the knife . . .
And, what am I in sex who shuttles
Obsessively from his
Stabs to recovery
In her small silent room?

The Looking Glass

Getting a man to love you is easy
Only be honest about your wants as
Woman. Stand nude before the glass with him
So that he sees himself the stronger one
And believes it so, and you so much more
Softer, younger, lovelier . . . Admit your
Admiration. Notice the perfection
Of his limbs, his eyes reddening under
Shower, the shy walk across the bathroom floor,
Dropping towels, and the jerky way he
Urinates. All the fond details that make
Him male and your only man. Gift him all,
Gift him what makes you woman, the scent of
Long hair, the musk of sweat between the breasts,
The warm shock of menstrual blood, and all your
Endless female hungers. Oh yes, getting
A man to love is easy, but living
Without him afterward may have to be
Faced. A living without life when you move
Around, meeting strangers, with your eyes that
Gave up their search, with ears that hear only
His last voice calling out your name and your
Body which once under his touch had gleamed
Like burnished brass, now drab and destitute.

Convicts

There was a time when our lusts were
Like a multicoloured flag of no
Particular country. We lay
On bed, glassy-eyed, fatigued, just
The toys dead children leave behind,
And we asked each other, what is
The use, what is the bloody use?

That was the only kind of love,
This hacking at each other's parts
Like convicts hacking, breaking clods
At noon. We were earth under hot
Sun. There was a burning in our
Veins and the cool mountain nights did
Nothing to lessen heat. When he
And I were one, we were neither
Male nor female. There were no more
Words left, all words lay imprisoned
In the ageing arms of night. In
Darkness we grew as in silence
We sang, each note rising out of
Sea, out of wind, out of earth and
Out of each sad night like an ache . . .

Jaisurya

It was again the time of rain and on
Every weeping tree, the lush moss spread like
Eczema, and from beneath the swashy
Earth the fat worms surfaced to explode
Under rain. It rained on the day my son
Was born, a slanting rain that began with
The first labour pain and kept me
Company, sighing, wailing, and roaring
When I groaned so that I smiled and stopped my
Plaints to hear its grief. I felt then that
Only the selfish had fears, that only
The unloving felt pain and then the first
Tinge of blood seemed like another dawn
Breaking. For a while I too was earth.
In me the seed was silent, waiting as
A baby does, for the womb's quiet
Expulsion. This then was my destiny.
Walk into the waiting room, I had cried,
When once my heart was vacant, fill the
Emptiness, stranger, fill it with a child.
Love is not important, that makes the blood
Carouse, nor the man who brands you with his
Lust, but is shed as slough at end of each
Embrace. Only that matters which forms as
Toadstool under lightning and rain, the soft
Stir in womb, the foetus growing, for,
Only the treasures matter that were washed
Ashore, not the long blue tides that washed them
In. When rain stopped and the light was gay on our

Casuarina leaves, it was early
Afternoon. And, then, wailing into light
He came, so fair, a streak of light thrust
Into the faded light. They raised him
To me then, proud Jaisurya, my son
Separated from darkness that was mine
And in me. The darkness I have known,
Lived with. The darkness of rooms where the old
Sit, sharpening words for future use,
The darkness of sterile wombs and that of
The miser's pot, with the mildew on his coins.
Out of the mire of a moonless night was
He born, Jaisurya, my son, as out of
The wrong is born the right and out of night
The sun-drenched golden day.

Composition

Ultimately,
I have come face to face with the sea.
In the beginning
the sea was only the wind's
ceaseless whisper in a shell.
But, lying beside my grandmother,
quite often I thought
that I could hear at night
the surf breaking on the shore,
The sea was only two miles away.
That was long ago.
Before the skin,
intent on survival,
learnt lessons of self-betrayal.
Before the red house that had
stood for innocence
crumbled
and the old woman died,
lying for three months,
paralysed,
while the thieving ants climbed her hands
and ate the cuticle.

Perhaps my innocence is not
all that lost,
if the stones still endure
and pieces of mortar lie scattered
in the field.
It may be
that in my heart

I have replaced love with guilt
and discovered
that both love and hate are
involvements.
But this only signifies growth
and, growth is natural.
The tragedy of life
is not death but growth,
the child growing into adult
and, growing out of needs,
discovering
that the old have black-rimmed nails
and scalps from which emanates
a sweet, mouldy smell.
In the years that followed
I was busy growing,
I had then
no time at all for the sea.
But,
there was off and on a seascape
in my dreams,
and the water
sloshing up
and sliding down.

When I got married
my husband said,
you may have freedom,
as much as you want.
My soul balked at this diet of ash.
Freedom became my dancing shoe,
how well I danced,

and danced without rest,
until the shoes turned grimy on my feet
and I began to have doubts.
I asked my husband,
am I hetero
am I lesbian
or am I just plain frigid?
He only laughed.
For such questions
probably there are no answers
or else
the answers must emerge
from within.
I have lost my best friend
to a middle-aged queer,
The lesbians hiss their love at me.
Love
I no longer need,
with tenderness I am most content.
I have learnt that friendship
cannot endure,
that blood-ties do not satisfy.
And so,
with every interesting man I meet,
be it
a curious editor,
or a poet with a skin yellowed
like antique paper,
a skin older than Jesus Christ,
I must
most deliberately
whip up a froth of desire,

a passion to suit the occasion.
I must let my mind striptease
I must extrude
autobiography.
The only secrets I always
withhold
are that I am so alone
and that I miss my grandmother.

Reader,
you may say,
now here is a girl with vast
sexual hungers,
a bitch after my own heart.
But,
I am not yours for the asking.
Grovel at my feet,
remove your monkey-suits and dance,
sing Erato Erato Erato,
Yet I shall be indifferent.
Not because of morality
but because
I do not feel the need.
But why worry?
What I am able to give
is only what your wife is qualified
to give.
We are all alike,
we women,
in our wrappings of hairless skin.
All skeletons are alike,
only the souls vary

that hide somewhere between the flesh
and the bone.
Skin a human being and he will
still breathe.
Starve a person, break his flesh
until he is reduced
to skin and bones,
and yet he will live
with attention.
But stripped of skin and flesh
the skeleton is dead
and most indifferent to the soul.

When I was home on vacation
some thirteen years ago
my grandmother asked me to spend
one night
in the old family-home.
We shall talk, she said,
darling,
we shall talk all night.
and,
in the evening,
she kept a lighted lantern
on the window-sill,
and sat up waiting for me.
The house was four hundred years old,
its rafters shook in the wind.
Those who thought my life precious,
cried,
do not go there,
we shall have no peace

with you sleeping under that
tottering roof.
My grandmother's lamp burned
all night
on the window-sill.
I know it is no use regretting now
or feeling ashamed.
I also know that by confessing
by peeling off my layers
I reach closer to the soul
and
to the bone's
supreme indifference.

Only those who like to listen,
listen.
What I narrate are the ordinary
events of an
ordinary life.
My first school-house
is now a brothel,
and
the ladies sun themselves on the lawn
in the afternoons
with their greying hair,
newly washed,
left undyed.
Who can say, looking at them,
that they are toys
fit for the roaring nights?
There must be something symbolic here,
but I do not

remember what.
I have gathered a few morals too
picking them
like wild flowers
on my way.
Husbands and wives,
here is my advice to you.
Obey each other's crazy commands,
ignore the sane.
Turn your home into a merry
dog-house,
marriage is meant to be all this
anyway,
being arranged in
most humorous heaven.
I have reached the age in which
one forgives all.
I am ready to forgive friends
their loving,
forgive those who ruined friendships
and those who forgave
and stayed on to love.
But I shall give a lot to get
one of my foes today
for a quiet picnic
somewhere.
Not having met for ages
we shall have so much to say.
But,
seriously, I must wake up,
come alive.
I tell myself

and all of you
who scan the mirror for that white
gleam in the hair,
fall in love,
fall in love with an unsuitable
person,
fling yourself on him
like a moth on a flame.
Let there be despair in every move.
Excavate
Deep, deep pain.
To be frank,
I have failed.
I feel my age and my
uselessness.
All I want now
is to take a long walk
into the sea
and lie there, resting,
completely uninvolved.

But,
rest is only a childish whim,
a minor hunger.
Greater hungers lurk
at the basement of the sea.
Ultimately
I will feed only the hunger
to feed other hungers,
that basic one.
To crumble,
to dissolve

and to retain in other things
the potent fragments
of oneself.
The ultimate discovery will be
that we are immortal,
the only things mortal being
systems and arrangements,
even our pains continuing
in the devourers who constitute
the world. Even
oft-repeated moves
of every scattered cell
will give no power
to escape
from cages of involvement.
I must linger on,
trapped in immortality,
my only freedom being
the freedom to
discompose.

From *The Old Playhouse and Other Poems* (1973)

The Old Playhouse

You planned to tame a swallow, to hold her
In the long summer of your love so that she would forget
Not the raw seasons alone and the homes left behind, but
Also her nature, the urge to fly, and the endless
Pathways of the sky. It was not to gather knowledge
Of yet another man that I came to you but to learn
What I was and by learning, to learn to grow, but every
Lesson you gave was about yourself. You were pleased
With my body's response, its weather, its usual shallow
Convulsions. You dribbled spittle into my mouth, you poured
Yourself into every nook and cranny, you embalmed
My poor lust with your bitter-sweet juices. You called me wife,
I was taught to break saccharine into your tea and
To offer at the right moment the vitamins. Cowering
Beneath your monstrous ego I ate the magic loaf and
Became a dwarf. I lost my will and reason, to all your
Questions I mumbled incoherent replies. The summer
Begins to pall. I remember the ruder breezes
Of the fall and the smoke from burning leaves. Your room is
Always lit by artificial lights, your windows, always
Shut. Even the air-conditioner helps so little,
All pervasive is the male scent of your breath. The cut flowers
In the vases have begun to smell of human sweat. There is
No more singing, no more dance, my mind is an old
Playhouse with all its lights put out. The strong man's technique
Is always the same. He serves his love in lethal doses,
For love is Narcissus at the water's edge, haunted
By its lonely face, and yet it must seek at last
An end, a pure, total freedom, it must will the mirrors
To shatter and the kind night to erase the water.

Blood

When we were children,
My brother and I,
And always playing on the sands,
Drawing birds and animals,
Our great grandmother said one day,
You see this house of ours,
Now four hundred years old;
It's falling to little bits
Before our very eyes,
The walls are cracked and torn
And moistened by the rains,
The tiles have fallen here and there,
The windows whine and groan,
And every night
The rats come out of holes
And scamper past our doors.
The snake-shrine is dark with weeds
And all the snake-gods in the shrine
Have lichen on their hoods.
O it hurts me, she cried,
Wiping a reddened eye,
For I love this house, it hurts me much
To watch it die.
When I grow old, I said,
And very very rich
I shall rebuild the fallen walls
And make new this ancient house.

My great grandmother
Touched my cheeks and smiled.
She was really simple.
Fed on God for years,
All her feasts were monotonous
For the only dish served was always God
And the rest mere condiments.
She told us how she rode her elephant
When she was ten or eleven
Every Monday without fail
To the Siva shrine
And back to home again
And told us of the jewel box
And the brocade from the north
And the perfumes and the oils
And the sandal for her breasts
And her marriage to a prince
Who loved her deeply for a lovely short year
And died of fever, in her arms.
She told us
That we had the oldest blood,
My brother and she and I,
The oldest blood in the world,
A blood thin and clear and fine
While in the veins of the always poor
And in the veins
of the new-rich ones
Flowed a blood thick as gruel
And muddy as a ditch.

Finally she lay dying
In her eightysixth year,
A woman wearied by compromise,
Her legs quilted with arthritis
And with only a hard cough
For comfort;
I looked deep into her eyes,
Her poor bleary eyes,
And prayed that she would not grieve
So much about the house.
I had learnt by then
Most lessons of defeat,
Had found out that to grow rich
Was a difficult feat.
The house was crouching
On its elbows then,
It looked that night in the pallid moon
So grotesque and alive.
When they burnt my great grandmother
Over logs of the mango tree
I looked once at the house
And then again and again
For I thought I saw the windows close
Like the closing of the eyes,
I thought I heard the pillars groan
And the dark rooms heave a sigh.
I set forth again
For other towns,
Left the house with the shrine,
And the sands,
And the flowering shrubs
And the wide rabid mouth of the Arabian Sea.

I know the rats are running now
Across the darkened halls,
They do not fear the dead,
I know the white ants have reached my home
And have raised on walls
Strange totems of burial.
At night, in stillness,
From every town I live in
I hear the rattle of its death.
The noise of rafters creaking
And the window's whine.
I have let you down
Old house, I seek forgiveness;
O mother's mother's mother,
I have plucked your soul
Like a pip from a fruit
And have flung it into your pyre;
Call me callous
Call me selfish
But do not blame my blood
So thin, so clear, so fine,
The oldest blood in the world
That remembers as it flows
All the gems and all the gold
And all the perfumes and the oils
And the stately
Elephant ride . . .

Nani

Nani the pregnant maid hanged herself
In the privy one day. For three long hours
Until the police came, she was hanging there,
A clumsy puppet, and when the wind blew
Turning her gently on the rope, it seemed
To us who were children then, that Nani
Was doing, to delight us, a comic
Dance. The shrubs grew fast. Before the summer's end
The yellow flowers had hugged the doorway
And the walls. The privy, so abandoned,
Became an altar then, a sunny shrine
For a goddess who was dead. Another
Year or two, and I asked my grandmother
One day, don't you remember Nani, the dark
Plump one who bathed me near the well? Grandmother
Shifted the reading glasses on her nose
And stared at me. Nani, she asked, who is she?
With that question ended Nani. Each truth
Ends thus with a query. It is this designed
Deafness that turns mortality into
Immortality, the definite into
The soft indefinite. They are lucky
Who ask questions and move on before
The answers come, those wise ones who reside
In a blue silent zone, unscratched by doubts
For theirs is the clotted peace embedded
In life, like music in the koel's egg,
Like the lust in blood, or like the sap in a tree . . .

The Inheritance

This then was our only inheritance, this ancient
Virus that we nurtured in the soul so
That when at sundown, the muezzin's high wail sounded from
The mosque, the chapel bells announced the angelus, and
From the temple rose the brahmin's assonant chant, we
Walked with hearts grown scabrous with a hate, illogical,
And chose not to believe—what we perhaps vaguely sensed—
That it was only our father's lunacy speaking,
In three different tones, babbling: Slay them who do not
Believe, or better still, disembowel their young ones
And scatter on the streets the meagre innards. Oh God,
Blessed be your fair name, blessed be the religion
Purified in the unbeliever's blood, blessed be
Our sacred city, blessed be its incarnadined glory . . .

Glass

I went to him for half an hour
As pure woman, pure misery,
Fragile glass, breaking
Crumbling . . .
The house was silent in the heat
Only the old rafters creaking.
He drew me to him
Rudely
With a lover's haste, an armful
Of splinters, designed to hurt and
Pregnant with pain. Why
Did I not cry then, broken glass, beware?
Why did I not tell him then that
I no longer care
Whom I
Hurt with love and often without?
With a cheap toy's indifference
I enter others'
Lives and
Make of every trap of lust
A temporary home. On me, their
Strumming fingers may
Revive
The fond melodies of a past.
I give a wrapping to their dreams,
A woman-voice,
And a woman-smell.
And I do not ever bother to tell,
I have misplaced a father
Somewhere
And I look for him now everywhere.

The Prisoner

As the convict studies
his prison's geography
I study the trappings
of your body, dear love,
for I must some day find
an escape from its snare.

The Stone Age

Fond husband, ancient settler in the mind,
Old fat spider, weaving webs of bewilderment,
Be kind. You turn me into a bird of stone, a granite
Dove, you build round me a shabby drawing room,
And stroke my pitted face absentmindedly while
You read. With loud talk you bruise my pre-morning sleep,
You stick a finger into my dreaming eye. And
Yet on daydreams strong men cast their shadows, they sink
Like white suns in the swell of my Dravidian blood,
Secretly flow the drains beneath sacred cities.
When you leave, I drive my blue battered car
Along the bluer sea. I run up the forty
Noisy steps to knock at another's door.
Through peepholes, the neighbours watch,
They watch me come
And go like rain. Ask me, everybody, ask me
What he sees in me, ask me why he is called a lion,
A libertine, ask me the flavour of his
Mouth, ask me why his hand sways like a hooded snake
Before it clasps my pubis. Ask me why like
A great tree, felled, he slumps against my breasts,
And sleeps. Ask me why life is short and love is
Shorter still, ask me what is bliss and what its price . . .

Gino

You will perish from his kiss, he said, as one must
Surely die, when bitten by a krait who fills
The bloodstream with its accursed essence. I was quiet,
For once, my tongue had fainted in my mouth.
It was July, a July full of rain, and darkness
Trapped like smoke, in the hollows of the sky, and
That lewd, steamy smell of rot, rising out of earth,
He walked one step ahead of me, the west wind leaking
Through his hair. And, I thought, if I could only want
Really, really want his love, we shall ride happiness,
Great white steed, trampler of unsacred laws,
If I could only dislodge the inherited
Memory of a touch, I shall serve myself in
Bedroom-mirrors, dark fruit on silver platter,
While he lies watching, fair conqueror of another's
Country, I shall polish the panes of his moody eyes.
And in jealous moods, after bitter words and rage,
I shall wail in his nerves, as homeless cats wail
From the rubble of a storm. But one only gets
The life one deserves, and dreams only such dreams as
The old soul can comprehend. I dream of obscene hands
Striding up my limbs and of morgues where the night-lights
Glow on faces shuttered by the soul's exit. And
Of ward-boys, sepulchral, wheeling me through long corridors
To the X-ray room's dark interior.
(O, the clatter of the trolleys, with the dead on them,
As loud as untimely laughter) And, of aeroplanes
Bursting red in the sky . . . I should be dreaming his
Peerless dreams, his dreams of sunlit villa and of fat

Half-caste children, lovelier than Gods and of
Drinking wine in verandahs, he and I, ageing,
And at peace, all disguise gone from us.

But I shall end differently, I know, our bloods'
Tributaries never once merging. It is
A dream-river, keep it so, the children are
Dream-children. Real ones never bear such splendent eyes.
This body that I wear without joy, this body
Burdened with lenience, slender toy, owned
By man of substance, shall perhaps wither, battling with
My darling's impersonal lust. Or, it shall grow gross
And reach large proportions before its end.

I shall be the fat-kneed hag in the long bus queue
The one from whose shopping bag the mean potato must
Roll across the road. I shall be the patient
On the hospital bed, lying in drugged slumber
And dreaming of home. I shall be the grandmother
Willing away her belongings, those scraps and trinkets
More lasting than her bones. Perhaps some womb in that
Darker world shall convulse, when I finally enter,
A legitimate entrant, marked by discontent.

From *Tonight, This Savage Rite* (1979)

A Phantom Lotus

The only truth that matters is
That all this love is mine to give,
It does not matter that I seek
For it a container, as alms
Seek a begging bowl, a human
Shape to envelope its wealth. Heed
My faith alone, all the rest are
Perishable, and as such but
Delusions. Any stone can make
An idol. Loving this one, I
Seek but another way to know
Him who has no more a body
To offer, and whose blue face is
A phantom lotus on the waters of my dreams.

The Caretakers

Yes, we stopped a step away from love,
Our hearts held back by will, for each knew
Well whom the other did desire
Though the desired were far and away.
There was little difference between us.
Each sought a severance from the past, now
Tightly packed like a valise, with faces
Turned into beloved junk, a short lull,
A kind of rest, but while I stood at
Hotel counters, filling in my name,
He took his trips, leaving body behind,
Laying all of it, neatly on the bed.
That scented, kinky head, that cold, closed face.
That furrowed brow and those poor pale limbs . . .
Our hands were timid in love-play, moving
On the other's skin, they knew they were but
Humble caretakers, for a short while allowed
To make their homes on another's lot.

Morning at Apollo Pier

Welcome me, lying down, dear love,
And remain so,
I shall shut the window
For, upward floats the leper's tremolo.
It is morning now at Apollo Pier.
There is a choppy sea, and on the pavement,
Like sleek birds freed from cages, beautiful men,
Inadequately loved, walking
To find a fatigue in their limbs.
You ask me what I saw today. I saw
The cripple stump along, hunger was both
His crutch and his limb. I saw the jerky walk
Of the very young, the baby's smile. I saw
The beauty of the ageing male, the face
Blanched in cool rooms, like flowers bleached by rains,
The haunches softened, the steel in the hair,
The knowledge in the eye . . .
They tell me, all my friends, that I am finished,
That I can write no more, they tell me
That the goose which laid the golden eggs can lay
No more, they tell me that your love is
A morass where I must sink, if not today,
Tomorrow. But, hold me, hold me once again,
Kiss the words to death in my mouth, plunder
Memories. I hide my defeat in your
Wearying blood, and all my fears and shame.
You are the poem to end all poems,
A poem, absolute as the tomb,
Your flawed beauty is my only refuge.
O love me, love me, love me till I die . . .

A Paper Moon

Your face is the moon left behind by yesterday's
Sorcerous night, white as a paper moon, pinned to
The curtain's blue, yesterday's prop for today's play,
A rhythm loping through grasslands of prose, a ghost
of happiness, yes, but a mood I'd rather not
Slip into, for I guard my frivolity,
Squirt gay laughter, retain with the night in my hair
A dark bravado and this inclement youth . . .

Ghanashyam

Ghanashyam,
You have like a koel built your nest in the arbour of my heart.
My life, until now a sleeping jungle is at last astir with music.
You lead me along a route I have never known before
But at each turn when I near you
Like a spectral flame you vanish.
The flame of my prayer-lamp holds captive my future
I gaze into the red eye of death
The hot stare of truth unveiled.
Life is moisture
Life is water, semen and blood.
Death is drought
Death is the hot sauna leading to cool rest-rooms
Death is the last, lost sob of the relative
Beside the red-walled morgue.
O Shyam, my Ghanashyam
With words I weave a raiment for you
With songs a sky
With such music I liberate in the oceans their fervid dances
We played once a husk-game, my lover and I
His body needing mine,
His ageing body in its pride needing the need for mine
And each time his lust was quietened
And he turned his back on me
In panic I asked Don't you want me any longer don't you want me
Don't you don't you?
In love when the snow slowly began to fall
Like a bird I migrated to warmer climes
That was my only method of survival

In this tragic game the unwise like children play
And often lose in.
At three in the morning
I wake trembling from dreams of a stark white loneliness,
Like bleached bones cracking in the desert sun was my loneliness,
And each time my husband,
His mouth bitter with sleep,
Kisses, mumbling to me of love.
But if he is you and I am you
Who is loving who
Who is the husk who the kernel
Where is the body where is the soul
You come in strange forms
And your names are many.
Is it then a fact that I love the disguise
and the name more than I love you?
Can I consciously weaken bonds?
The child's umbilical cord shrivels and falls
But new connections begin, new traps arise
And new pains
Ghanashyam,
The cell of the eternal sun,
The blood of the eternal fire
The hue of the summer-air,
I want a peace that I can tote
Like an infant in my arms
I want a peace that will doze
In the whites of my eyes when I smile
The ones in saffron robes told me of you
And when they left
I thought only of what they left unsaid
Wisdom must come in silence

When the guests have gone
The plates are washed
And the lights put out
Wisdom must steal in like a breeze
From beneath the shuttered door
Shyam O Ghanashyam
You have like a fisherman cast your net in the narrows
Of my mind
And towards you my thoughts today
Must race like enchanted fish . . .

From *Collected Poems* vol. I (1984)

Speech

Lyre strings,
Earth's network of veins
And piano keys,
Each livened pulse;
Wind's finger tips
Twang,
Percuss the pulse,
Rain but drums,
And trees,
Their repose
Aquiver,
Rot within,
The lichen
Their only speech.

The Lunatic Asylum

There is a light
Burning all through the night
At the lunatic asylum,
An unshaded
Bulb, shaped like a teardrop,
Hanging from the dead white ceiling
Of the hall, to
Chase the moody shadows
From the inmates' beds so that they
Lie with open
Eyes, and yet without
Fear; it burns harshly, a sun that
Does not ever
Set but harsher still burn
The lamps in their skulls, those lights that
The bromides or the electric whiplash
Of every week cannot put out.
Those large and hot
Insomniac lanterns
Under which grey spectres dance in
The sepulchral
Ballrooms of their minds. No,
Do not pity them, they
Were brave enough to escape, to
Step out of the
Brute regimentals of
Sane routine, ignoring the bugles, the wail
Of sirens and
The robots' stern bark
Hup, two, three, hup two three, hup two . . .

Fear

A lidless eye,
Day bellowing into day
Without a night between,
A noonday sun come at last
To stay . . .
Substance,
Bereft of shadow,
A scream,
a swift knife-gleam,
Deafens the unwarned
Human ear . . .

The Sea at Galle Face Green

Like a half burnt corpse was
That once splendent city;
Its maimed limbs turned towards
The smoke-stained sky, and
Even the small leaves of
The Kathurumurunga
Stopped their joyous tremor
While the sea breezes blew.
No birdsong in the trees
Only the stomp of boots
Worn by the adolescent
Gunmen ordered to hate.
Did the Tamils smell so
Different, what secret
Chemistry let them down?
Was there a faint scent of
Jasmine in their women's
Hair? But how did they track
Down the little ones whose
Voices rose each morning
With the National Flag
And its betrayed lion.
An affectionate beast
A king of kings, let down
By his son. How did they
Track down the little ones
Who knew not their ethnic
Inferiority?

The city was grey
And every window was
Shut. Fear was in the air
As the corpses smouldered,
Fear and a stench sweet as
That of raw cashew nuts,
Roasting. The sea did its
Duty as usual at
The Galle Face Green, without
A sign of fear, without
A sign of shock or pain
It patrolled the empty shore.

After July

After July, in Colombo there were
No Tamils in sight, no arangetrams
Were held in the halls, no flower-seller
Came again to the door with strings
Of jasmine to perfume the ladies' hair.
Like rodents they were all holed up in fear,
Their smell began to resemble the rats',
A mixture of dung, copper and potash.
They were the hunted; they cowered behind
Doors, in the murky twilight of their rooms,
The whites of their eyes, glimmering like pearls.
Hitler rose from the dead, he demanded
Yet another round of applause; he hailed
The robust Aryan blood, the sinister
Brew that absolves a man of his sins and
Gives him the right to kill his former friends.
The dark Dravidian laid his three year old child
On his lap. Little mother, he cried, close your eyes and sleep.

Smoke in Colombo

On that last ride home we had the smoke
Following us, along the silenced
Streets, lingering on, though the fire
Was dead then in the rubble and the ruins,
Lingering on as milk lingers on
In udders after the calves are buried,
Lingering on as grief lingers on
Within women rocking emptied cradles.
They stopped us, a somnambulistic
Daze was in their eyes, there was no space
Between us and their guns, but we were
Too fatigued to feel fear, or resist
The abrupt moves
Of an imbecilic will.

The Moon

Each night the moon cools the sun-cooked
Goodies of the world, pats and shapes
With weathered hands the dough of grief,
And swathes gently the embarrassed
Loneliness of middle age, so
That again the desired words
Are said on balconies, and faded
Eyes glitter with hope. The leper
Dreams of his own wedding day; with
Unflawed arms and legs he sports on
His bridal bed, and his girl is
So beautiful, her head thrown back
In laughter. Not even the new
Planetarium that smells of
Chrome and rexine can change the moon
And its ancient ways, its measured
Tread. It is a trained circus dog
That shall never miss its hoop.

Endlessly healing, it waits for
The new day's wounds, just a witch who
Fattens on others' mishaps, lying in
Wait behind the mountains for its
Appointed hour, then emerging
Round-faced like a female seer to
Seek out the sad and if all else
Fail, prescribing a draught of
Lunacy to remove the pain.

Requiem for a Son

A cold wind blows from the airfield today; the mother trembles
With unease, remembering again the son who
Did not return from his play. He had told her once, the air is
My father, it will not betray me but it wrung out of his
Throat his first cry of terror and scattered him over the trees
Among the white and purple bougainvillea bloom, hurled his
    innards
With the wantonness of breakers that toss in the messy
Treasures of the sea. The public liked what it saw, the mangled
    son,
A silenced lion wrapped in a flag, the dry-eyed mother; it
Offered its blurred pity and hurriedly left to print the story.
Her laments were silent, her heart was a throne room locked
    for years
Where she walked alone with a mirror in her hand. Death is
Ordinary. To live on an earth built upon layers and
Layers of bone requires an extraordinary
Courage, to walk the corridors of this prison and note with
A quiet joy the saplings bursting from the cracks in stone and
Know for certain that life will go on. He was impatient with
Old wisdom's slow narrations, his dreams had wings to lend
    them speed,
I must do it, he cried banging a clenched fist against a palm,
I have no time at all to waste. Grass has already grown on
The dirt track that returned him each day to his home, his ears
    filled with
The drone of planes, his limbs chilled by the morning dew.
    Can he hear
From where he is, the words of the living? Words are a harvest

Gleaned from granite, they are dry and can give no comfort. I
was
The maker of your world, said the mother, but when you died
you seemed
To take away mine. Night is a woman in widow's weeds,
Reminding of wet graves and wreaths and my sleep is the
hangman's
Troubled pre-morning slumber, yes, grief burns coldly like a
moon,
I live and wither, you die, but blaze with a wondrous life, for
A mother's love often fashions a kind of eternity.

No Moon at My Village Home

They close in on me, those sleep-walking trees
With owls on their shoulders, pensive ones with
Feathers ruffled by the wind, and the pond
Lays on me its cold unbleached shroud, joining
In the conspiracy. On the dust of
Windowsills I spot the signatures of
The patient ghosts, the trees have thatched a darker
Roof; the moon of cities, the moon of vast
Rice fields sprinting past the trains, is nowhere
To be seen. Only the fireflies light up
Our porch, only the silence tells me that I must
Stay . . .

A Souvenir of Bone

The fire was red blood that night, I remember the house
Burning down, the slow folding of its limbs, the crackle,
And the children carried in sleep, asking dully from
Under the trees, what is it. Since then the littlest fire
Has had for me a very secret incantation,
A message that I have heard and held in a haunted
Mind. The fugitive flame of the evening lamp on
The patio was the seed of the fire tree, the seed
Of a gorgeous death. What was the wind, I asked, where lay,
Its roots, what gave it nourishment, and there was always
And always the fire answering me, the wind is
Cold hunger. Its roots lie deep and in the sea. How often
Have I have wished as child to peel the night like old
Wallpaper and burn it, to hold at monsoon time
The wounded wind in my arms, to lull it back to sleep!
As child I was led into cheap imitation, I was clothed
In white khadi and branded on my skin. It was
My pretence that earned for me a niche in the house
Three free meals and the khaddar uniform. My desires
Were many, if granted freedom I knew they would burn
Down like tongues of flame, the monastic peace of my home.
The ancient lusts are blinded in the mind, they stagger
Through the light of day as mad men stumble on sidewalks
At noon. Once as in a dream I sat with him at
A restaurant, it was called 'Palettis' then, and under
The balcony the gaunt Anglo Indian played his violin.
Do you know this song asked my friend and I shook
My head. Oh it was such a laugh! How could he think
That I knew any song? Helpless with the cutlery
I put aside my plate and wept. His nature was then

Water, mine was fire. He had no doubt at all, and
I had many. I told you my nature was fire; it was
Greed and ingratitude. If I am a sinner, please
Forgive my sins. If I am innocent, forgive my
Innocence. In his wild arms where I rest today
There will once be the gross air, nothing else. They will
Burn me then on a log and pick for each grieving son
A souvenir of bone. Rob me, destiny, if you must,
Rob me of my sustenance, but do not, I beg
Of you, do not take away my thirst . . .

Woman without Her Shadow

She lay still, her open eyes two cartwheels
Stunned to a sudden halt. It seemed to her
At times that years had sped by since she had
Despatched her shadow to him who needed
Her, though she was older by years, and ill.
One day at last it returned, and raising
Herself from her pillow she cried, you have
Changed, I would not have recognised you, had
I met you outside my home, you are dark,
toasted black, as though some hell-fire had clasped
You to its bosom for a while. It replied
Smiling, I was busy, I had no time
To breathe, I walked along the streets at dusk,
Holding his hand in mine and sipped coffee
In a South Indian café where each waiter
who served us looked like another Jiddoo
Krishnamurthy, and lay against him all
Through the winter nights; like a flag hoisted
On a mountain range till then unclaimed.
Unseen, was my cheek against his,
And my heart against his, yes, I kept him
Yours for a spell and now I return,
Longing for home and rest. Planets slid like
Dice from players' hands, hurtling into space;
Their silence boomed in her ears. She ran down
The fearsome stairways of the sea. Like
A wild Westerly suddenly set free
She moved with terrible ease, and in
The musty bracken of the sky the witch

Azaleas bloomed for her
And the unnamed birds of every heaven
Burst into song; there was then no disputing
Her strength or her legitimate role
But, from another city, lonelier
Than hers, he moaned in afternoon sleep,
Dreaming once again of her dying day . . .

A Half-Day's Bewitchment

Ultimately the house and I became one. My heart's door
Swinging ajar with each vagrant breeze was the wrought iron gate,
Its hinges rusted from disuse, creaking to let
A traveller in, perhaps a postman delivering
A cable addressed to an occupant, dead for several
Years; and, in that alcove where the bats with human faces
Resembling the shrunken heads of the African warriors
Killed and trophied by their Massai enemies hang,
Hangs also my soul which remote controls my poor body
So that with only a half-day's bewitchment
The beautiful ones are reverted to stranger rank, for
I am also the sea that roars behind the house, roars out
Its passion at the high tide hour; but, later the ebb arrives
To tall a different tale. I have, like the sea, some silt
At the core, some junk, the leavings of ships floundered in the night,
A few bones, a beer can or two, a compass with needles
Missing. But azure remain our dreams, both the sea's and mine
And all the experiences worth remembering come
To us only in dreams which we forget when we wake
Face to face with the sun as eternal as truth itself . . .

Death Is So Mediocre

Life has lost its clear outlines. Or else, I may
Have gone half blind, its ritzy splendours stealing
The light from my eye. The night, forever
A garbage collector, tearing grubbily
The wrappers off many a guilt, remains
A dubious ally. All the rest are lying morgued
With that hazy past. And, yet invitations
Come from strangers who proudly string me between
Starched serviette blooms at their tables. And, after
The drinks are drunk and the food eaten, when asked
To speak I find my poor mouth turn into an
Open cavern, ransacked bare, by burglars
Of thoughts and suddenly wealth and lust seem like
Languages once learnt but now forgotten. Death is
So mediocre, any fool can achieve
It effortlessly. For those such as me the awful
Vulgarities of the final rites are not
Quite right, the slow unwrapping of the carcass,
The many paltry, human details that must disgust
The aesthete, the flabby thigh, the breasts that sag,
The surgery scar, yes, it would indeed be
Of no bloody use believing in my soul's
Poise when the paid marauders strip me of that
Last unbleached shroud and ready me for the fire.
Like an elephant not bidding goodbye while
Taking off for that secret edge of forests
Where they slope into a sure but invisible
Sea, I shall go too in silence leaving not

Even a finger print on this crowded earth,
Carrying away my bird-in-flight voice and
The hundred misunderstandings that destroyed
My alliances with you and you and you . . .

The Sensuous Woman

The sensuous woman must choose her illness as she
Chooses her clothes to suit her own style, a certain
Delicate condition invisible to the eye
Inspiring awe and tender sympathy
So that she may lie, a martyr's halo
Lighting up her pillowcase, under rugs
Of cashmere or silken quilts, limbs flaccid
As a baby's, skin cool as a rose, and
The visitor tiptoeing in with his
Offerings of flower or fruit must inhale
The sandal in the air, the scent of cotton wicks
Burning themselves out in lamps which her room
Mysteriously seems to hold always,
Although bare of such exotica, and must stoop
To kiss the back of an idle hand, unused
To chores all except that of kindling love.
And, as day and night as one tide after
Another roll away, an ocean's vast
Languor seizes her blood, the fences between
The state of life and death fade, and nailed
To the pleasant cross of Being she straddles
The handless clockface of eternity.

Flotsam

We were the homeless, he and I, the floating ones
Who recognise swiftly another of the tribe
By that certain hunger in the eye, a slight
Narrowing, for, although brimming with a desert sun,
It fancies it sees an oasis; the mirage
Greenly reflected in each lonely cornea,
And, so together we stumbled so clumsily
Into lust. But pushing his urgent limbs away
I fought to regain my body's poise till he cried
I love you, you've no need to be afraid of me.
When at last he left, scolded, sent away, alone
On the white desert of my sheets I wondered if
I should have fought at all to save this dubious
Asset, my aloneness, my terrible aloneness.

The Cart Horse

Of late my words have worn
Thin, my speech resembles
The jagged gallop of
A cart horse that needs to
Be re-shod and perhaps
Given rest, for, poor thing,
Its roads were arduous
And its burden always
Too heavy. An old horse,
If lucky, dies on road,
Flopping on its side with
Pink foam spurting from its
Twisted jaw and four of
Yellow front teeth showing.
The not so lucky are
Taken out and shot, for
The old and decrepit
Waking at times from their
Senile slumber, neigh, loud
In hunger, and parents
Of the rich who sit with
Their keepers on benches
Beside the sea wall, with
Cataract on their minds
Tremble at this sound, for
No reason the old ones
Purse their mouths and tremble.

Herons

On sedatives
I am more lovable
Says my husband
My speech becomes a mistladen terrain
The words emerge tinctured with sleep
They rise from the still coves of dreams
In unhurried flight like herons . . .
And my ragdoll limbs adjust better
To his versatile lust . . . he would if he could
Sing lullabies to his wife's sleeping soul
Sweet lullabies to thicken its swoon
On sedatives
I grow more lovable
Says my husband.

I Shall Not Forget

My illness wove for me a grey shroud.
Within the wrap
Like a blighted seed I moulted
Rotting to the core.
Even my third eye could see nothing familiar;
At midnight hour whose black bird feet beat
A tattoo on my patio
While the murky sea wrung its white hands at my gate?
Dull life, blindly adorning tomorrow's corpses
With glitter and silk
Or long clawed birds of death
That stayed by me while I watched my father die.
His smoky eyes had died long before he died.
The earth had entered the skin
Soundlessly, days before the burial,
Settling its dung.
And its river silt turning black the blood.
I pulled back the eyelids once to look
They were dead fish eyes with a cataract mist.
I shall keep shut that hopeward door
I shall not escape
Let the budgerigars build their nests in my winter voice
I have seen death
And I shall not forget . . .

Advice to Fellow-Swimmers

When you learn to swim
Do not enter a river that has no ocean
To flow into, one ignorant of destinations
And knowing only the flowing as its destiny,
Like the weary rivers of the blood
That bear the scum of ancient memories,
But go swim in the sea,
Go swim in the great blue sea
Where the first tide you meet is your body,
That familiar pest,
But if you learn to cross it
You are safe, yes, beyond it you are safe,
For even sinking would make no difference then . . .

From the *Indian Literary Review*
(vol. III, no. 2, April 1985;
previously uncollected)

Cochin's Jewish Quarter

Walking the cobbled lane in Cochin's Jewish Quarter,
I watched the evening's sun slant against shuttered faces,
Pale, gleaming at dark doorways like a bouquet
Of some unfragrant bloom, and walked on, uneasy as
I always seemed to be in unsmiling towns, hearing
An old dog moan, resting its head on the windowsill.
And glancing in, I saw a man lie there, slowly dying
With a twitch of his loosened mouth and a rolling of
His eyes; there was no one else within the room but the dog.
He was perhaps dying of some fearsome pox alone
In a cluttered room with just one window that faced
The shadowed East. I wished I had a mirror then to offer
Him the face of the sun, the small cold face of an autumn sun
Or, at least the courage to sit holding his poor
Failing hands. Coward that I was and civilised
To suit the age I entered an antique shop
With a neat rapid stride and in the rasping voice
Of the greedy, bargained for a Ming . . .

The New Sinhala Films

Yes, indeed cowards have common sense, they place
Stepladders under the secret slats in ceilings,
Once meant only for the yearly cleaning up,
Arrange their passport, visa and wedding ring
In a bundle along with a first-aid kit
To make the getaway as easy as it
Ever can be, under the most distressing
Circumstances of their being creatures of
Indian origin, Tamils or cousins of
Tamils, during this season of legalised
Hate. Politics have dried up emotion, and
The close friends I have among the Sinhalese
Wait till dusk to visit me and they wisely
Talk only of the new cinema as though
Nothing has happened in the recent past but films.
But the stench of burning flesh is still within
Our nostrils, the silence of the curfew hours
Still hums in our ears and so good-naturedly
Smiling becomes a difficult feat although
Resignation came easy enough to us,
Born revolutionaries, the erstwhile addicts
Of freedom. We close our windows at six
And sit facing the TV stand. At night in
Bruised sleep the Sinhalese pour gasoline
On our heads to burn us down, and as corpses
Devoid of the power to scream we wake with open
mouths, trembling uncontrollably in those long
Pre-dawn hours, dipped in the milk of waxing moons.

When at last we return, if at all we do,
Dodging the speeding army-truck or perhaps
The accidental shot, we shall not ever
Discuss the disgusts of the past but shall only
Talk brilliantly of Dharmasiri Bandaranayake's
'Thunveni Yamaya' and 'Arukgoda's Monarateuna' . . .

Hairpins and Rubber-Bands

All through the past sobering years, krait-like
I shed dead cells of skin and found at last
In the oldest of bonds most attractive
Legitimacy. And yet, when I comb
To unsnarl my greying hair at night, soothed
By solitude, your slim body's pressure
On mine is felt, all is remembered then:
Your leonine tresses, the sparkle of
That smile and the passion that lingered throughout
A jasmine-scented season. Yes, I jinxed
Your life, even the ring I gave you was
A vice biting into your flesh and its
Yellow topaz grew cold and murky as
Tragedy after tragedy struck and
Death was a bystander watching, while cheek
To cheek we stood, unshed tears glistening
In our eyes, I was never cruel enough
Or even noble. There was then no choice
But to flee your orbit in haste, put your
Love away and grow older, and silent.
The hair that sailed backward does not move now,
When I walk the same darkening shore,
Although the wind rises from the sea as before.
I've learnt the use of hairpins, rubber-bands . . .
In virginal sleep your body's slimness
Intrudes and a vast hunger racks my limbs like a storm.

From *The Best of Kamala Das* (1991)

Mortal Love

Fidelity in love
is only for the immortals,
the wanton Gods who sport in their
secret heavens and feel
no fatigue. For you
and me, life is too short
for absolute bliss and much too long
alas, for constancy.

A Journey with No Return

Desire swims as a dolphin does
in the rivers of my blood tonight,
desire sports as a dolphin does
with sudden leaps and lurches.
My limbs are tense with embarrassment,
I am ashamed to raise my face to yours.
I long to put aside my sacred vows
and long to forget the sweet domestic past.
With an amnesiac's level gaze I shall walk
by this scorching love made new . . .
There are only two furlongs to reach your home
but it would be a journey with no return,
for the fire that I bear to warm your bed tonight
would burn down the ramparts of my home.

Delhi 1984

The turbans were unwound, the long limbs
broken and bunched to seem like faggots
so that when such bundles were gifted
to their respective homes the women
swooned as their eyes alighted on a scarred
knee or a tattooed arm. The scriptural
chant sounded like a lunatic's guffaw;
any God worth his name would hasten
to disown these dry-eyed adherents
of the newest cult. No breast was left
unfondled, no ripe cunt overlooked
as terror, fleet of foot, did rampage
the sedate suburbs, while in the queen's
funeral pyre the embers lay cooling.

The Ferry Hour

Yes, the trees are being erased now
And the bright sea lassoing the shore,
The hills paling in the blue, the birds
Hiding in the bough, the cow, the dog
Beside the door, and even the lined
Face above mine. I hear the bough sing,
Has the sea stopped its noisy game then?
Someone is holding my fingers tight.
Someone is sobbing beside my bed.
But it is the ferry hour at last
Like bales and bales of bleached white cotton
I shall stack my thoughts on the boat's dark floor,
With chilling finger tips I have erased
Even the face with its weeping eyes.
On the laundered sheets of memory
I shall squat all night to reach that shore.

My Father's Death

Only the insincere shed tears
At my father's death, those who came
To get photographed with the corpse,
He was the most important man to die
In Calicut since Vasco trod the sands at Kappad.
Looking around on both sides of roads
The people stood, pre-arranged, to watch
The flower-bedecked hearse pass,
And the police with polished batons directed the traffic's orchestra.
Only the men were allowed to join the convoy,
We stayed behind and sat near Mother
Who was too fatigued even to weep.
Our house seemed then like a theatre, deserted,
Bits of tinsel and petals littered up the porch.
For twelve days and nights we had kept a vigil,
Gazing into his shut face he had shrewdly traded
In his pain for a coma that was thick like a fog,
He was like a puppet attached to its strings.
Thin rubber tubes grew like tubers
From every orifice and a strange beast howled
From within his chest as though in pain.
Mother said with a sob, it's not his death that I fear but this,
Oh God, I cannot bear to hear it again and again . . .

Only those who lost their monthly Baksheesh
Wept at my father's death,
He was generous with his money,
As generous as I was with love.
There was a cloud of tension between us.
I brought him shame, they say. He brought me on each

Visit banana chips and words of reproach.
I feared my father.
Only in that coma did he seem close to me,
And I whispered into his ears that I loved him,
Although a bad daughter, bad wife and bad mother, but in the task of loving the bad ones were the ablest.
You should have hugged me, father, just once,
You should have used kind words just once a year.
You gave my sons hundred rupee notes,
You purchased their devotion but my price was too high
For you, your wallet could not hold
Abstract currency. Talking and talking
Of family bonds will not grow them, you know, father . . .

Vrindavan

Vrindavan lives on in every woman's mind
And the flute luring her
From home and her husband
Who later asks her of the long scratch
On the brown aureola of her breast
And she shyly replies
Hiding flushed cheeks, it was so dark
Outside, I tripped over the brambles in the woods . . .

The Anamalai Hills

There are no clocks here at Anamalai, no cock crowing
the morning in, as the muezzin's call from cold mosques,
only the mist so absentmindedly lingering on, long past
the dawn's legitimate hours and the invisible
bird's crazed cry, occasionally from the mosquito tree.
From somewhere within my heart
the mist ascends, the mountains awake,
perhaps the rains are over and the swamps are dry again.
It had been only the mist rising against the hills,
clinging and unclinging as it must always do, it had
no kinship with the hills, no blood-tie,
yes, it was at best a minor collision, nothing else.
I hear the mountain speak: I was alone, I am alone, I will be alone . . .
With the languor of queens, *enceinte*, the fog ascends
the stairways of the sky. Anamalai stands undisturbed.
Wrapped in the shrouds of betrayals,
the woman walks alone. The mountain seems deaf-mute,
but the flesh of her spirit is but its flesh,
and, her silence,
despite the tumult in her blood,
its destined hush.

The Anamalai Poems*

I

How often have I trod these mountain paths,
The mist, like tattered pennants beckoning
to me; yes, from each city I lived in,
each dusty small town I stole out often
to walk this winding road, laying aside
my poor body that had perhaps no home,
no territory to call its own. Mine
was a somnambulistic tread, so soft
that not even the labourers heard it,
who walked with hooded heads among the trees.
There was none to see me or recognise
but the bird hidden in the silver oaks
a bird that cried out my name, a shrill cry
that pierced the silent sombre fog slowly
ascending the lone Anamudi peak . . .

II

There were nights when I heard
my own voice call me out
of dreams, gifting such rude
awakenings, and then
expelling me from warm
human love, unaccustomed
fare for one such as I,
a misfit when awake.

III

If I had not learnt to write how would
I have written away my loneliness
or grief? Garnering them within my heart
would have grown heavy as a vault, one that
only death might open, a release then
I would not be able to feel or sense . . .

IV

Ultimately we come to know
that for us there is only one
claimant whom by mistake we call
death, obsessed as we are by our
physicality, restrained
by the eyes' inadequate power
to perceive beyond the farthest
precincts of truth. If only the
human eye could look beyond the
chilling flesh, the funeral pyre's
rapid repast and then beyond
the mourner's vanquished stance, where would
death be then, that meaningless word
when life is all that there is, that
raging continuity that
often the wise ones recognise as God?

V

At times I feel that I hide behind my dreams
as the mountain does, behind the winter's mist
I cannot look the day in the face as once
I did, with gumption or confront myself and
declare, yes, old girl, I have sure let you down.
They called me a winner, for, with words I did
weave a wondrous raiment fit for Gods and with
nimble footsteps climbed the stairways of my thoughts
finding even the heaven's portals ajar.
My songs echoed in stranger's dreams, in unease
they stirred in their sleep and sighed. Yes, often, poets
gatecrash into the precincts of others' dreams
as Gods and Goddesses do many a time
in unsolicited magnanimity.

VI

I have cut myself adrift from those who professed
to need my love and can now have freedom even
if it be that insecure one of the boat
bereft of rowers, oars or sails, yes, only
the blood's moorings have any relevance but
they rest in ancient graveyards now turned into
municipal playgrounds where over layers
and layers of brittle bones the booted legs
of adolescents kick a football around
or, in the southern wing of the ancestral
estate where the coconut trees have nailed down
the matriarchs' bosoms with thirsting roots.

No, not for me the beguiling promise of
domestic bliss, the goodnight kiss, the weekly
letter that begins with the word dearest,
not for me the hollowness of marital
vows and the loneliness of a double bed
where someone lies dreaming of another mate
a woman perhaps lustier than his own.

VII

If someone would only remove the sun
from my way I would not have to face
another sorrowful day but I would
lie then in kind nights' embrace, soothed by its
blinded compassion while its groping fingers
would anaesthetise my private terrors . . .
If someone would coax the night to linger
beyond its legitimate phase, I shall
not wake with tear filled eyes again or look
down the chasm of another sad day
to perceive each and every time only
the debris of the past night's genial dreams.

VII

The longest route home is perhaps
the most tortuous, the inward
path you take that carries you step
by weary step beyond the blood's
illogical arrogance, yes,

beyond the bone and the marrow
into that invisible abode of pain,
yes, that deathless
creation tethered to your self,
and constantly struggling to wrest
itself free, tethered to your soul
as your shadow is to your form,
your Siamese twin no surgeon
can cut away from you. Other
journeys are all so easy but
not the inward one, the longest
route home and the steepest
descent . . .

IX

Life yields its true meaning only
in early youth or in weary
age. The middle is an opaque
glass pane, muddied by fingerprints.
In meaninglessness, trapped, I must
so remain and taste the outer
rind of human pain and the seeds
of mirthless laughter.

X

There is a love greater than all you know
that awaits you where the red road finally ends
its patience proverbial; not for it
the random caress or the lust
that ends in languor.
Its embrace is truth and it erases
even the soul's ancient indentations so that
some unknown womb shall begin to convulse
to welcome your restructured perfection.

*I, III, V, VI, VII, VIII and X first appeared in an eight-poem sequence as I, II, IV, VI, V, VII, VIII in *Indian Literature*, vol. XXVIII, no. 2 (March–April 1985).

From *Only the Soul Knows How to Sing* (1996)

A Hand like a Bonsai

No, not again, dear one, that tiresome game
Which I played so long, so well, but they filled
My forests with white fire while I did try with
Tears to douse it until a terrible
Wisdom settled on my heart, heavy like
A tomcat and the soft pleas froze on my tongue.
No, not again, the season is long past
And gone. The long necked birds shrill from the trees.
The copper shield bearers are in haughty bloom.
I look through the sea as if it were a
Window, the unfinished houses block my view.
Through the scaffoldings I see the blue. The sky
Has a white patch, a cloud pasted clumsily
On its wan cheek. At night, when my family
Falls asleep, I pull their sleep over me
Like a silken quilt and let my aloneness
Heal. I recollect no matings then, no young
Ardour, only the white snow country of
A hospital sheet, and over it, like
A dark bonsai, my father's beautiful hands
Which chilled to marble, later, among
The wilting wreaths.

Fathima

Fathima has cancer. A breast removed,
and lulled by the pay-wards' soft palaver,
she fattened around that seed of death like
a pearl around its grain of sand, a pearl, ripe
for plunder, with the sheen of a gull's wing
and the autumnal brilliance of the sea.

Feline

We have so few symbols to use as motifs
in our creations. We weave the fabric
of our art, settling and unsettling an ancient
design, the earth, the sun, the yellowed leaf, pain,
illness, death and of course some inconstant love.
Amidst these basics stretch out without an end
the indeterminate hues and shapes of myriad
unknowns, the vacancies that held us before
the womb's embrace, the spaces that shall contain us
after the closure of graves or the red fire's
rapid repast, the deciduous ferns that
we ignored while we wandered plucking short-lived
bloom. There is a sea wailing beneath the sea,
a sky behind the taut drapes of our firmament,
a rain that rains hard and long within the summer-rain.
Another lives in me, I fear, a twin left unborn,
unnamed, unacknowledged, bitter with defeat,
and, she with her new-moon eyes stabs my face
and turns me so often, half human, half feline.

The Motif in the Mirror

Outside, the rain had ceased. We closed the verandah door. All the blue
Lights were on. How shall I describe that first embrace, you have not seen
The many mirrors in his room? When we embraced, we fell in their
Cerulean pools as a deathless motif, repeating, repeating,
Repeating this reflection of a reflection, this shadow of
A shadow, this dream of a dream, and I knew him then by knowing who
I was, and knew myself more by knowing who he was, but he said,
Rising from my side, it is eight, get up 'sweet wife' I'll take you home.

Too Late for Making Up

Father, it's too late for making up with you
The time for debates on honour is over now
You won, didn't you? You left me without goodbye
Or a look that told of your feelings for me.
All I could do was light an oil lamp
And place it beside your head
After they had wrapped you in off-white khaddar
And laid you on our drawing room floor.
Everyone who knew you brought you a wreath
Either of lilies or of rose,
At last to spare your tired legs I cried
Leave them standing against the wall.
You turned cold on the drawing room floor
Colder than your heart ever was, father.
The house was filled with red-eyed people
And someone read the Gita
Some weeping would have looked real nice
It is done in the best of families you know.
All I could do was sprinkle eau de cologne on you
And decorate your chest with flowers,
She is the daughter that went astray
I heard someone whisper
The one who caused him the greatest pain
And look at her now, acting solemn.
Should I have loved you, father
More than I did
That wasn't so easy to do
If I have loved others, father,
I swear I have loved you the most.

The Bison at the Water's Edge

Who says a marriage must mean only two?
The clement climate of mine was due
Not to one man alone, but two,
Two dissimilar co-tenants
In one cramped room.
One the kind side of a blade
The other the cutting edge
Yes, the other was indeed hard.
In his small eyes were desire and death
But I took roots at his windowsill
To become a wild stubborn cactus,
Believing, believing, in the rain
What secret purpose I followed
Walking to his door
To sway together, to swing together,
Beside that mirror in the corridor.
But later, back at home on my legitimate bed
Arms that could not grasp him
Grasped no sleep either
I heard the murmuring fall of silence
Like white sand falling
And during the longer nights
I saw the moon's halo age and rust.
But why recount a dead tale,
It is now quite off the point.
Under sand piles of silence lie buried my footprints
Narrow tracks of the prey
Leading to his lair
Each day his lust renewed me

Each day he rent my virgin loins . . .
I wiped a tear away
Before I rang his door bell.
On that last determined day
I said I've come to bid goodbye . . .
After years and years, one morning
Returning with my library books
I ran into him
It was sudden, yes, very sudden,
Like the swift slap of the summer's sun
On a sequestered pool
A tremor in his smile, a hello,
I had not realised till then that being
No longer a god,
And no more the dark bison at the water's edge,
He had shrunk to an old man's
Meek proportions
And that having so recently lost a son,
His small eyes now held only hurt and pain.

Larger than Life Was He

The living must ultimately
triumph over the dead
and outlive them in moderate calm,
In twenty weeks
my grief gave way to faint stirrings of guilt.
In the gauzy sleep of dawn
I had not lain against him
for fifteen years or more
I had tried as satiated wives did
to wean him off desire
My celibacy flowed like a river in spate
between the twin beds in our room
There are no memories that enthral,
no fond phrase capsuled in thought,
It was never a husband and wife bond.
We were such a mismated pair,
Yet there were advantages, I admit
he was free to exploit and I was free
to be exploited.
We were quits at every game we played
I could have been Sita to his Rama
had I been given half a chance.
I reared three sons,
he was too busy to watch them grow
but he it was who wore the faded face
that they recognised as their father's.
His was the heavy tread
heard on the gravel at dusk
He peered into his office files

till the supper turned cold
and the children got up to sleep
I cannot recollect a film
a play or a concert he took us to
or a joke which together we shared.
He was like a bank locker
steely cold and shut
or a filing cabinet that
only its owner could unlock
Not for a moment did I own him.
Only a few bed-bound chores
executed well, tethered him to me.
Emotion was never a topic
brought up in our home
although for long it remained
as grist for the tales that the night
and I, combined, produced.
Do I miss him?
Of course, I do, for larger than life
was he. I miss that brusque voice
sending out the trays
hugging their manuscripts
meekly as unwed mothers did
their illegitimate offspring
I miss his censoring my daily mail
his screening each phone call
and the insulation of his care.

A Feminist's Lament

An ideal woman, they said, was but
a masochist. Trained from infancy
to wear the flannels of cowardice
next to her skin, trained to lie inert
under a male, committed by vows
to feed her, clothe her and buy for her
the 1000 sq. ft. flat with a loft
for storing the debris of passing years.
I was never that ideal dream. Nor
did he buy the flat for me.
Widowed and diabetic
wrinkling like a bitter gourd
not even death can perfect me now.
What was courage worth
at the very end?
Even Phoolan the dacoit queen
finally threw down her guns
to settle for weekly orgasms.

Next to Indira Gandhi

Next to Indira Gandhi my father I feared the most
He was the one who told me when I was five
That dark children should only wear white.
He was the one who had no time for me
When I was growing up,
Lost and lanky with braces on my teeth
And tortoise shell glasses covering my eyes.
He was the one who attended the Rotary lunch
Every Tuesday without fail
And signed away fat cheques for charities
But when I saw him each day for half a minute
Climbing down the stair
He stared past me
His office problems kept his thoughts away from us.

Father, I ask you now without fear
Did you want me
Did you ever want a daughter
Did I disappoint you much
With my skin as dark as yours
And my brooding ways?
On Saturdays you saw the matinee show at Metro
Seated in the third row, right?
The Smiths were with you or another pair
As sleek as they
And white
Twice I sat with you; Mrs Smith had insisted on it,
The films were both Laurel and Hardy stuff
You chose my clothes for me

My tutors, my hobbies, my friends,
And at fifteen with my first saree you picked me a husband.
I am grateful
For choosing for me a man
And a life of suburban dullness
Brightened with embroidery and crochet work
And the Thursday Cookery class
But it was not the rightmost groove for me
It wasn't my cup of tea.
I know I let you down, father,
But you have punished me enough, haven't you?
We are quits today. You are dead, nobody fears you now
And I, freed from fear at last,
Feel no relief at all. I feel dead. More dead than you . . .

For Cleo Pascal

In Canada
it is autumn time
the maple leaves
red as drying blood
may not last out the week

I grow visible
more visible here than there
the inescapable visibility
of the darker race
peopling a white God's world
How would He have guessed
the traumas of the black?

The sky and the wrinkling sea
peer through veils of grey
I am the loving intruder
in love with Atwood and her land
Would even my love seem dark,
dark and therefore a wee bit
sinister?

Only the trees seem glad to see me
as if I were their kith and kin
I take on their characteristics
as the days one after another pass by
while I wear this land as an overcoat
warming my breasts and belly
I begin to look like its trees
my skin dries like the bark of a birch

my hair smells of spruce
There are creatures in the undergrowth
I smell the swamp and the loam

The birds are hiding
they hoard their melodious cries
in the lockers of silence
Canada's silence is different
from other silences known
It is a gigantic deep-freeze
in which sounds lie wintering . . .
Of one thing I am certain
the forest and I,
we have something in common,
we do not speak French.

Smudged Mirrors

Thoughts do not seem to jell . . .
Words turn their backs on me
as strangers do, embarrassed
by the intimacy of a stare.
A bird scratching in the mud
with its flight a mere memory.
Smudged, its vision of frothy seas
and of rice stalks parting
as the wind passes by
A smudged mirror yielding
a blue and yellow blur
Wings turned to torn limbs
and the heart beat timorous
For what bizarre purpose I live on
my calves forever aching,
and traitors of senses deceiving?

From *Kavya Bharati*
(No. 10, 1998)

A Divining Rod

A divining rod
I misplaced somewhere
is my poetry
I am now mute and
irreversibly remote
I am beggared
by its loss
It seems like the withering
of a limb
with blinded eyes
I search for the treasures
of my past
I cannot recognise
my friends or my foes
I am a mute remnant
of what I was
the embers of a fire
someone other than I
put out

From *Kavya Bharati*
(No. 12, 2000)

Wild Honey

You gave me a jar of wild honey
I gave you my love
My love is so much
like honey collected from the forests

Several springs lie dissolved in it.
Each night the
weight of your body
wearies my arms.

But you lie against another
woman's body in a town
far away from my home

How long is it
since you and I began
to run round the rim
of a circle seeking
out one another?
I cannot guess
Today
I do not even know
if I am pursuing you
or if you are pursuing me.

The thought that
morning is leagues away
makes me lie
each night sleepless.
Was it in another
life perhaps remote that
I heard for the first time
your soft voice, your
gentle words?

Why do you stand
silent outside my door?
Your silence thumps against
the walls of my heart.

Who built a shrine
at my feet?
Prayer bells trill in my ears.
I am a river that flows
on, unaware of its
limitations. On an
evening after the sun had
set you visited me.
It was then that it flowed
as if in spate.
Who can now stem its flow?

At which fated hour
did my arid life
turn into a plaything
meant only for you?
You were a scholar.
You roamed around
scattering shreds of moonlight.
Today you are wise.
You burn like the Sun.
But I tremble fearing
that one day you might
discover the transience of
our love. Am I
to get scorched by the sun?

We had as
weapons only our religions.
We had to abandon
them on the floor
before we could embrace
each other.

Why do you
stand before me with
the troubled face of a
convict? Why do you
tremble in fear before
the one who loves you?
I admitted you into
the interiors of my
home only because you
were an innocent.

Are you forever
seeking in me the lost treasures
of youth? Oh pilgrim
late in arriving, your
only duty is to give
me my last drink of water.

Your finger tips
are blunted for you chew
your nails. With blunted
fingertips you strum my
heart strings, you liberate
strange melodies. This is to
be our honeymoon. We
joined the suicide squad
ready for self-sacrifice

And if love is not
a sacrifice what then
is its meaning?

The Mask

How can I love him without causing
his mask to crack, a mask more cherished
than his naked face, one of intense
piety that glows like an auburn sun
against the horizon while the wine
of his tremulous voice is poured again and
again into goblets of adorers' ears?
Transient as the splintering sun
in the moving river beside his home
was his love and transient the leap
of desire in his burnt sienna eyes
But how shall I survive the aftermath
of love and the sudden awakening
in him of reasons, the silence banked
as snow in the Nokia he gifted a month or two ago
returning from a Gulf-land to my impatient arms?

The Maples Are Green Still

Perhaps in slumber lies
as yet unemerged
the tarnished copper of their leaves
and my beloved's too
I remember the red hot rages
that awakened
under my gypsy lips.
Was there ever a woman
able with words to describe the splendours of her
lover's body?
Ya Allah
import for us
for my silent one and me
from the heavens above
a language that is versatile
and conveys love's anguish
and the concomitant bliss
with words that resemble the sighs
of moments when we cling
and afterwards uncling
in leisurely detumescence
Ya Allah
I thank you once again
and again and again
For this gift of a man
who is now my sustenance
the draught I thirsted for
and the sole raiment
for my nudity, both my body's
and my soul's.

The Separation

Among the maples
and the pine
among the cedar
and the birch
descends the hurricane
of my desire for you
an untimely one that must
shake down the limbs of trees
and bruise the forest,
these hills . . .
Your stricken eyes
tinged red
bother me my love
In the stillness of a Canadian night
I hear the resonance
of your voice
calling out my name
and the body lying disciplined
under the eiderdown trembles
recalling our last embrace
You asked for a maple leaf
to keep pressed in a book
If this anguish lingers on,
lingers on and on
I shall bequeath you
my heart, chilled and red
so like a maple leaf in autumn
to keep pressed
between the pages

of your prayer book
a relic to remind you of
promises left unfulfilled
and happiness dreamt of
but not realised.

I Dare Not Gaze Again

Don't turn your face
or look at me, dear one
I dare not gaze again
into the depth of sequestered pools
Behind the layers of cold skin
may lurk sleeping suns
that might rise out of the water
like naked leprechauns
to beguile
to please
I dare not play the games
adults seem to play
the game of enticement
the game of laughter
and the final one of abandonment.

A Moment's Pain

Words pelted at me
in sudden
casual malice
scar the veneer of my pride
till it crouches like a stray
beside the sewers of
dark consciousness
Within a flawless form
the invisible trappings hurt
and I see myself a cripple
crutches under arms
begging with eyes
for kindness
For love . . .
I must arise
I must depart
to the yellow lights of
prosceniums
the din of crowds
closing in on me
and the deafening applause
the embrace of rustics
the unlearned ones
who give unquestioningly
their love
and their underarms' smell
to these I must return . . .
To the maples
taking their own time to redden
to the elephantine rocks

to the pines and the birches
to the glimpse of
silvery lakes
to the thrumming air
of the forest
to the birds crying out
their creator's name
I discover that I do not
belong
and that I shall not ever belong.

Scalpels

You gave me no wedding ring
or even a promise laced with hope
You held me in your arms
and passed on your cough to me
After half a year has passed
the cough still lingers on:
Love too endures, I hope . . .
On the phone at your hospital
your voice, a steely scalpel
probing my innards,
drives me to the farthest
periphery of your world
I shiver like an outcaste
I taste the cold metal of defeat
Perhaps only in my arms
you soften
adopt a human form
At such moments you serve me
ladles of silence
in a leisurely way
the silence of old trees
adorning your family home
which remember you as a child
the silence of birds that roost
invisibly in the trees
the silence of distant hills
in the wake of a storm.

Alien Territories

Today I leave Merrily's home
for a land that's far away
where I shall not smell the
birch leaf and the spruce
Here I was the owner of my time
each tranquil hour my own
none to make claims on the vitality
and the depleted assets of age
none to plead with sunken eyes
for permanent sustenance
or for a roof above her head
Ya Allah
how long can I aid you
in your ordained bondage of love?
How brief my earthly sojourn
how eternal thy pursuits
If you have visible feet my Lord
I shall press my lips to them
I shall dampen your toes
with my tears
that seem to flow
from a remote interior
that is perhaps within me
and yet seems alien
a territory bequeathed
a territory unearned

From *Kavya Bharati* (No. 15, 2003)

The Passing of a Typhoon

Hearken to the cry of crickets
In the summer air;
Crickets in bamboo groves,
Crickets in the ripened fields of rice,
Perhaps a forerunner,
This strident clamour,
Of the typhoons to pass my way
To the vast cyclone of the mind
Where cruelty ploughs
The bloodred soil
And ill winds from nether worlds
Sow nightmares to suit the age.
Emotions still exist
But battered out of shape,
Shallow sequestered pools,
A muddy waste that a past
Shared with offspring and a mate
Left behind,
Its meagre debris,
Its messages still undeciphered.

The Circus

This is my guess, right or wrong.
Words written out by poets
And prophets are wise
But wiser still remain the truths
That are not written.
Dig into the nest of tap-roots
To unbury the revelations
That sprout their heady bloom
On the other side of earth.
Travel inwards devouring Time
Burrowing into the myriad layers
Of the planet's body
Beyond the skin
Beyond the bones and the marrow
To the nadir of life
The hot, dark cellar
Of loneliness.
Old age is a distorting mirror
One cannot recognise oneself
In its glaze.
Who would have paid the price
To come as a tired spectator
Carrying the child within
To this ultimate circus?

From 'Personal Poetry', Unpublished MS (2004–05)

At God's Loom

He found himself woven
as silken woof
for the warp of my existence.
A certain loom had worked
overtime, yes it was
Allah's handiwork
Neither his nor mine.

(19 May 2004)

The Snake Shrine

Desire burns
like the wick we lit
at the family's
snake shrine
years and years ago.
Somewhere within
the silken folds
of the labia minora
a flame lingers on
resisting age
and defying
mortality . . .

(May 2004)

Gracious Allah

Compulsive speaker of truth
I thought you guileless
but you used his
brown riveting eyes
To lure me on.
And afterwards, his
perfidy made me want
to flee, to return
to the arid tracts
I had traversed,
the deserts of the soul.
Sand more sand
and idols carved of stone
even a grandmother's
bedtime tales of valour
etched on the pewter
of memory faded, yes
indeed, dear one
when I left my land
for yours
carried no heirloom
no luggage to slow down
my flight
no remnant of a life
that had had almost all
but love . . .

(signed, Suraiya, 22 May 2005)

From *Encountering Kamala* (2007)

The Palmyra Tree

Ammalu Amma,
ancestress of mine,
prone to writing verse,
cut into long strips
the stiff leaves of
the palmyra tree and
engraved the stanzas
with a stylus.
The grooves were stained
with the juice of a leaf
the name of which
I do not now remember.
The manuscripts tied
with cords and stored
in her slanted desk
of rosewood did not fade
with time. What made
the new rich buyer of
my land cut down that
ancient tree? What pittance
could he have earned
from its carcass?
It was said, long ago,
that a Yakshi, a celestial
ogress, lived on the tree,
who descended at dusk,
disguised as a maiden
to lure an unwary male
into her abode, and then

after a tumultuous mating
devoured his flesh and
flung down his bones.
Padmavati, the sweeper,
swore that she had many
a time swept away with
her broom the Yakshi's
leavings: bits of bones.
Some nights when strong
gales rose from the Arabian
sea, lying beside my sleeping
grandmother I had heard
the loud flapping of
the Palmyra leaves and
the sound of bones cracking.

Volcano

Quite often unrecognized
as poetry, your scribbles
embrace the world
oblivious of the stale tenets
of prosody you must
write on,
draw from the most
ancient of wells,
draw on and on till
the water shows brown,
brown of dregs,
brown of sediment,
brown of the blood
coagulating in
the lab-bound syringes.
Continents pull up their
drawbridges, they do not
expect a ruler or even
political dignitaries to pass.
They wait for you to enter,
bare feet falling, lighter
than a yellow leaf's falling
in the autumn breeze,
your breath faintly fluttering
like moth wings among the bloom,
you serve honey disguised
as some kind of lethal poison
its effect takes a long while

to show. Truth has a slow,
delayed reaction. It is
the distant rumble
of a fevered volcano.

A Kind of Fishing

I shall cast my nets
in the ruffled sea
of my past
and shall fish out poetry
that is neither glad
nor sad
but can cut
precisely the gut
to wake you
out of dreams . . .

The River Saraswati

Which untaught language
do I speak in my dreams
when I meet the dead,
still so dear to me who
form the backdrop of this faded
life? Their lips do not seem
to move; neither do mine.
But as the river Saraswati,
long beyond history, vanished
into the earth, perhaps our
humdrum human speech too
went under. But invisibly
the grand river flows
towards its ordained sea.
We can sense its swell,
its impatience, its lust.

Researchers

When you live long enough
and progress as a poet,
friends fall away,
either in envy,
or in disgust.
Only a motley bunch
of researchers arrive
banging on your door.
Looking this way,
that way, they resemble
scavenging birds
hungry for their prey.
They peck at your nerves
as though they were
spaghetti, edible.
They are ravenous
for tasty titbits;
many split open your bones
and lick the marrows off.
Poets are edible
material, even one at
death's door can provide
a research scholar
a memorable feast.

Alzheimer's

Alzheimer's disease
is a spider
deadlier even than
the tarantula.
It weaves its web
within the brain,
a web rugged like
wrought-iron
and thought-proof.
My mother
for seven years had
Alzheimer's.
It looked out
through her eyes
although she was
silent as a safe
plundered bare,
emptied of memories,
her disease talked.
Like a Buddhist monk,
it said
life is sorrow . . .

Fame

Fame is merely the smoke
the kitchen-chimney emits
when you cook a meal.
Do not be awed by it
or give in to pride.
Smoke is ordinary,
all it does is
cloud your vision.

From *Closure* (2009)

The Roosting Time

Where did the days go,
the minutes
the seconds?
To think that there was
no life at all
and that I dreamt it all?
The pregnancies,
the pain,
chortling babies
on my lap!
The babies
grew into strangers,
strange foes who carried
in their scabbards
sharpened words,
strangers who bore
in their hearts
great padlocked doors.
No, I have not entered
their interiors
for fear of falling
into an abyss of scorn.
I run away from
living things
while my feet swell
like eco-unfriendly
sweet potatoes
grown out of season.
I disown these balloons
of feet, my pretty parts.

I disown
these ugly protuberances.
If I gain some respite,
some strength
I shall not write wills
that bequeath
my meagre possessions
for fear of amusing
my biographers—
few bangles of gold,
a dented medal
won at school. Words
of a stray madness
scribbled in the night
using my felt pens
a biographer sent by courier.
She alone sends me
any gifts by courier,
from Quebec's Laurentians.
This may be because
she finds significance
in my responses.
Being my biographer
she is in no hurry
to write the final chapter
or my epilogue
that deals with my end,
the ignominy of being
undressed by strangers.
Strange hands
prodding
probing

for evaluation
of personal essence.
The soul will baulk
at human touch
and turn away
in fright.
Who did I belong to?
Whose asset was I?
There are bellies
and bellies
and all empty.
I am a series of
emptiness
assembled
without care,
a monarch's feast
gone waste . . .
I shall not be a friendly corpse.
If vultures eat me,
they shall perish
of a stomach ache.
I taste of insulin,
I taste of bromides
and codeine.
I devoured life,
chewed it around
like a mint gum
till it became
insipid rubber,
offal of what it was
when I had believed
in the possibilities

of love.
I was the one
always in a hurry,
in a hurricane's haste,
a Cinderella
of the present
twenty-first century.
Do you see me
or do you avert your eyes
when I pass your way?

Radha's Dream

Oh Krishna
I did not for a moment believe
that you were a dream.
In your embrace
how could I have noticed
the seasons changing,
the leaves falling,
and the rising mist?
Spring was within me
and immortal love
when you entered
I became your home,
a woman doomed to live as stone.
There had been till then
no music in my world.
I was slowly moving
towards old age
seeking the reason
for creation.
How could I, poor Radha,
believe that you were
but a dream,
was paradise to be,
yet another dream?

A Tethered Goat

Tethered to a pillar of
ignorance
I am an animal
that can only go round
and then turn back to go
round again.
The bomb blasts stop
me in my tracks. I do not understand
much of today's psychology
or its lactating mother
they chose to call philosophy.
I cannot bring myself
to hurt one to whom
I was not introduced.
I cannot feel the hate
so much in vogue today,
I am somebody's pet,
an outdated plaything
now abandoned for time
to step in, and in
a leisurely way destroy.
I am the goat
who in hunger ate
Pluto's *Republic*,
Kalidasa's *Shakuntata*,
Gurdjieff's analysis
of his own cult
and, of course, Walt Whitman's
Leaves of Grass.

I do not qualify
as wholesome meat
for the butchers
who come by surveying the scene.
I look as sickly
as sickness itself can be,
none would want to eat me
for dinner.
This I consider a boon
in this century of
bigotry, arms' bazaars
and haphazard killings . . .

Thrombosis

A lone thrombus
driving into an artery,
a clot that lost its way,
nothing more.
The moment, the last of
the very last,
wipes out memories.
The fences are down
the past and the present
merge and dissolve.
The faces around
reshape themselves to hang
as lit lanterns
above the dying ones.
Merry Xmas,
happy new year
here I go
leaving all.
Going is easy,
as easy as arriving.
When directions cease
to exist
pain and pleasure
taste the same,
one becomes one's own
collapsing axis,
you become your own
collapsing axis.

Coral Snake

Larger than the noon itself
was its gift
of a vision,
a sprawling nightmare
of a dim lit lawn,
a hedge
and my sons, still
children, among the rugs
of light
and a coral snake
on the hedge,
orange and black,
yet another peril
I must avert
while they move on,
on chubby legs,
unafraid
and in silence
I look on . . .

Pune,
green city
have you forgotten me,
forgotten I ran across
the glade, my sons in tow,
forgotten the mixed laughter?
I return,
old and too ill to walk.
While I lie on my bed
watching the sky,

its whorls that curl
and uncurl
I cannot decipher
its varying codes
but soon the mosquitoes
descend,
in hordes they descend . . .

Light a Bonfire

If you wish to kill me
do not attempt the killing
with a knife or gun,
burn my books
one by one,
build of my poems
a bonfire in your backyard,
let the fire rise and bloom,
let the flames rage
as I used to once rant and rage
at an erring husband.
Jealousy being a traditional
weapon neither rustic
nor quite urban,
just an unease
sliding along the innards.
Was he not satisfied with
the splendour of my hair,
the firmness of my adolescent limbs,
the perspirations, muskrat scent?
You frighten me, he said once,
with your childish anger,
and your poetry.
Poetry brought me nothing
more than a sense of rejection,
a knowledge of the perishable body
being worthier than the mind
in the ordinariness of the marriage game.

I Shall Live On . . .

After wearying centuries
when my name and form
cease to be
keep your ear
close to the ground
I shall be the thrumming
of the impatient seed within,
the plant pregnant with
next summer's bloom,
the sorrowful wail
woven with the breeze—
hearken to its grief—
the thready whorls spiralling
down the sky,
the shimmer of blue wings
against the ocean's blue.
Yes, listen to the sea
Don't you hear me sigh?

March of the Mercenaries

Love was the only religion
I ever recognized. We
arrived with love-words, it became
even more relevant. I made
our anxieties mine, the rhythm
of your breathing, the frequent ache
of your calloused feet, and then
without unease
your religion too.
But very soon
I discovered that Allah was
not your Master; fearing the wrath
of your commanders you left me,
your march was that of a soldier
who belonged to a regiment
of mercenaries, your courage
that of a robot's remotely controlled.
Where is the paradise
we together dreamt of,
gardens filled with nightingales' song,
angels sliding down the blue skies?
I do not any more hold you
in my arms. An ache lives within,
an ache that does not seem to die . . .
The crumbling of my world thumps
against my ear, the trees descend,
flowers drop, ripened fruits fall
and the nightingales'
nests fill with eggs.

When an egg breaks
I think of a tomorrow
that ends like
a foetus that dies, open-mouthed.

A Timepiece

I was so ill
so ill, so frightened
that I neglected all,
neglected my own self
more than all.
Now I lie as a ticking timepiece
under a quilt
beaten by a sense of loss.
What a waste
of energy—a cloudburst
of intense fantasy!
I never learnt
to compromise,
I thought I would
learn from Islam
a clean way to compromise—
I did not.
I am hard as a nail
on the cross—
not the original cross
they hung Jesus on—
there are myriad Iscariots
lurking in the dark
waiting for the cock's
third crowing.
But I am too shabby
for resurrections.

Pritish Nandy, a man
of meagre talent called
my books pulp-fiction.
No, not even a maggot can
grow out of the debris
of my crucifixion,
not an ant alive
shall peer out of my viscera.
Do not put my body
in any coffin of wood,
the embers of my corpse
will burn holes and smoulder.
If I marry an ordinary man
I had hoped I would become
ordinary,
insulated against scorn.
Who would want to
marry me?
I am such an eccentric!

When I loved,
I became pure love,
when I lost
I became pure loss,
nothing else.
There is no beautification
in suffering,
I shall break open
my mind
and display the viscera.
I shall hold an exhibition
at the Chitram Art Gallery.

Chitram does not invite me
any longer to inaugurate
their shows,
conversion to Islam
bothers them all.
Muslims and Hindus,
both factions are bothered.
I am no Mother Teresa
eligible for canonization.
I am no Amma
ready to embrace all.

I am some kind of a worm
now laid under
the microscope.
My fame itself
is in doubt,
it's crisscrossed with blunders.
I am the son
of Eleanora Duse
said Heinrich Heine
or, was it Gordon Craig?
I forget names.
Will one of my sons dare to say
I am the son
of Kamala Das?
My wayward search for love
made me seem ridiculous.
All searches are wayward,
there is grace
only in repose.

The Magnolia

Like a magnolia bent with
excessive bloom was my frail form
burdened with desire. But
you humbled me with coarse words, made
me feel old and inadequate.
I cannot buy youth at any
pharmacist's. Take yourself away
from the sunny orbit of my life,
impotent male who with a grin
of pride calls himself a sadist.
You have sullied the purity
of my perspective. You have slain
love with knife-thrusts of verbiage.
Have I been perverse till now, drawn
to a small-town symbol of fair
commonness, a Paleolithic
toy made out of clay? Why did
the cranes, their wings agleam, rise
from the ripened rice fields and fly
to dim my landscape and my sky?
Why did a rain of misery
overflow the horizon's rim?
You could not ejaculate but
I ignored the flaw. You spewed
anger, an orgasm singular
and strange. I owe nothing, I don't
owe anybody a thing but perhaps
I do owe something to poetry.

When I walk the nights away
sleepless with a tread lighter than
a soul's, I break the backs of
roaches, the brittle shells of egos,
but that too is a poet's fate.
Illness and medications sprout
a kind of verse oddly perfect.
One gets only the hell well deserved,
thank God for that. My lover
is a chess piece I must sweep off
the board to bring order where
disorder roams. I shall not have
a heavy hand on my bosom,
a greying head against my knee,
I shall no longer feel thirst or
hunger. I shall swallow gusts of
sweet air and chew down the slats of
yellow, yellow, yellow sunshine . . .

Editor's Note and Acknowledgements

In making this selection, I have followed the chronological order of the appearance of these poems in book form and, in some cases, in journals such as *Kavya Bharati* and the *Indian Literary Review*. An exception, however, has been made in the case of the Anamalai poems. In January 1985, Kamala Das wrote fifteen poems for the sequence, including the title poem 'The Anamalai Hills'. Eight of these poems were first published in *Indian Literature* (March–April, 1985); seven from this sequence, except No. 3, along with three of the remaining poems were reproduced in a rearranged order in 1991 in *The Best of Kamala Das*. Three more unpublished poems, numbered 9–11, from the original sequence, exist in Kamala Das's MS on the *Mathrubhumi* letterhead.

The eight poems from *The Old Playhouse and Other Poems* included here have appeared earlier in the *Illustrated Weekly of India*, *Quest* and *Opinion*.

Seventy-three new poems were published in *Summer in Calcutta* and *The Descendants*, together. Further new poems, together with previously published poems, appeared in all subsequent volumes except the one from Australia. *Encountering Kamala* (2007) printed sixty-three new uncollected poems under different sections: *Laurentian Poems* (2000), *Cinderella in Disguise* (2005), *I Shall Live On* (2007) and *Pune Poems* (2007), besides thirty-two poems from *Only the Soul Knows How to Sing*. In *Closure*, except for three poems—'The Magnolia', 'March of the Mercenaries' and 'Radha's Dream'—the rest are edited/corrected versions of those that appeared in *Encountering Kamala*. And of the sixteen poems

poems included in *Wages of Love*, five first appeared in *Encountering Kamala*, and 'Nightmare at Noon' as 'Coral Snake' in *Closure*.

Many of the new poems in *Encountering Kamala* were, unfortunately, printed with typographical errors. A comparison of the versions in *Encountering Kamala* with those in Kamala Das's MS suggests that these typographical errors resulted from a misreading of the poet's handwriting.

In order to avoid double editing, I have preferred versions printed in *Closure* and *Wages of Love* to the ones printed in *Encountering Kamala*, except in the case of seven poems. The title and the names of the artists in 'A Timepiece' are as in Kamala Das's MS.

Encountering Kamala, an omnibus edition, published by Andrew Arkin, an American friend of Kamala Das, also includes photographs: *Laurentian Drawings: Sketches Created in the Canadian Mountains* (2000) and *Poetic Sketches* (2005). One of these sketches, *Manon de Lescaut*, is reproduced here. While preparing this edition, I learned from the poet Robert Hershon (email of 30 July 2014) that, sadly, Arkin had died five years ago and that his son Jason had dissociated himself from all the books his father had published.

~

This selection of poems brings to a full circle my interest as a critic in the poetry of Kamala Das. On 28 February 1988, when I was serving as Professor in the University of Kashmir, Srinagar, the poet sent me, through Gulab Vazirani of Arnold-Heinemann, a file which included her unpublished poems and prose writings. This was to enable me to prepare a volume of selected poems. For various reasons related to the exigencies of my situation, I was unable to fulfil this commission then. Later, in August 2006 in Kochi, Kamala Das gave me a copy of an MS of unpublished and published poems. After her move to Pune, Jaisurya Das sent me on 16 August 2008 a copy of an MS of fifty-three poems, with a note: '. . . Kamala wanted me to send you her Pune poems . . .'

The present volume can be seen as an effort to fulfil that trust.

Preparing this volume has also meant a personal, nostalgic revisiting of the 1960s and 1970s for me. My 'discovery' in 1966 of Nissim Ezekiel, Kamala Das, A.K. Ramanujan and Zulfikar Ghose was not guided by the curriculum in the University of Delhi where I studied and taught; however, the stimulus of being at the University of Leeds during the 1970s impacted my subsequent writing in this area. I recall with gratitude the encouragement I received then (while I researched into the poetry of Robert Graves) from several scholars such as A. Norman Jeffares, William Walsh, who invited me to give lectures to his class, and Arthur Ravenscroft, who published several of my articles in the *Journal of Commonwealth Literature*. Sadly, these friends are no more but their pioneering footprints are still visible.

My supervisor, Geoffrey Hill, was also a source of inspiration and support. Two other friends I first met in Leeds in 1971 animate the present. I would like to express my appreciation to Dieter Riemenschneider for lively conversations about India and Indian literatures; to Bruce King for the exchange of views on Indian poets during our respective peripatetic careers—in Leeds, London, Canterbury, Delhi, Srinagar, Graz, and through correspondence—and for contributing to the *Indian Literary Review*.

I owe special thanks to P.P. Raveendran, V.C. Harris and Meena Pillai for providing useful information; and to Jaisurya Das and M.D. Nalapat for supporting the venture and answering my queries from time to time.

Thanks are due to Kristian Fredén, librarian, the Nobel museum, and Mikael Svanberg, the Nobel library, Stockholm, for promptly answering queries and providing a copy of Kamala Das's work published in *Artes* and *Artes International*; to Sufian Ahmad, librarian, Sahitya Akademi, New Delhi; and to Paul Love and the Study Centre for Indian Literature in English and Translation (SCILET), The American College, Madurai, for sharing information from their Kamala Das archive.

I would like to express my sincere thanks to Chiki Sarkar at Penguin for supporting the proposal, to R. Sivapriya, my editor, for her patience, encouragement and meticulous editing, and to Tanvi Kapoor for her excellent copy-editing of the text.

I am grateful to Graham and Barbara Parry for their warm friendship, generosity, and animated conversations about poetry, history and the arts. I should like to thank Barbara Schmidt-Haberkamp for our lively discussions relating to our past and prospective collaboration on Indian writers. To Suresh Kohli, thanks for providing useful material, and of course for many a shared interest. Thanks to Isha Chandrika Kohli, for being among the first readers and for the shared enthusiasm for poetry, and to Vijaya John Kohli, for insightful perspectives, cheerful optimism, companionship and love.

Paderborn, October 2014